C000241570

**Battleground**

# THE AFFAIR AT NÉRY

# Battleground Europe

# THE AFFAIR AT NÉRY

PATRICK TAKLE

*Series editor*
Nigel Cave

Pen & Sword
**MILITARY**

First published in 2006 by
LEO COOPER
an imprint of
Pen & Sword Books Limited
47 Church Street, Barnsley, South Yorkshire S70 2AS

**ISBN 978 1 84415 402 9**

A CIP catalogue of this book is available
from the British Library

Printed by Redwood Books Limited
Trowbridge, Wiltshire

*For up-to-date information on other titles produced under the Leo Cooper imprint,*
*please telephone or write to:*
Pen & Sword Books Ltd, FREEPOST, 47 Church Street
Barnsley, South Yorkshire S70 2AS
Telephone 01226 734222

# CONTENTS

# Introduction by Series Editor

The Official History gives four pages to what happened at what is now a rather charming village near Paris. 1914, Volume I, Chapter XII begins with this sharp engagement, which is officially called 'The Affair of Néry', and dedicates four pages to it. Compared to much bigger engagements, the interest it aroused then – and continues to do today amongst those interested in the Great War – might seem to the disinterested observer to be disproportionate. I would argue that it does deserve at least a high proportion of the fame it has achieved.

It was an engagement where great heroism was shown, which of course is true of many of the other actions fought by the men of 1914. In this case, however, we know a lot of what happened on the ground from the large number of eyewitness accounts, from both sides of the battle. It is an action that involved cavalry, a much attacked part of the army in the years subsequent to the Great War, condemned as being archaic by the outbreak of hostilities.

What Néry does show is that cavalry correctly used (and supported logistically) had the potential, at the strongest, of being a war winning arm. What the campaign of 1914 shows is that the Germans made poor use of their cavalry and had never trained it effectively in the immediate pre war years for the type of operations that faced its army in the opening moves of the war.

It is also an opportunity for looking at the capabilities within the BEF in 1914. Time and again significant operations on the battlefield had to be conducted by low ranking officers and by NCOs. When one reads an account of an action such as this at Néry it shows what depth there was in the original BEF – a depth that became evident to me as I was studying the short, very sharp action at Le Cateau. Because it is a small battlefield, relatively unscathed by modern developments, involving small numbers of troops, it is an action that can be relatively easily understood and the problems facing both sides appreciated.

Thus this new entry into the *Battleground Europe* series is to be welcomed for providing a clear guide as to what happened in this insignificant corner of France, well away from the customary battlefield tourers' stamping grounds. It is another example of what courage and training can achieve in enormously difficult conditions.

Nigel Cave
*Collegio Rosmini,* Stresa

# INTRODUCTION

In 1914, the British and French forces began the war in a mood of high optimism. The British had the confidence of professionals who were used to policing a world wide Empire. The French also had their colonial experience, and were committed to the philosophy of the attack. In the east of France they immediately attacked vigorously to recover the provinces of Alsace and Lorraine, which had been lost to Germany in 1871. In the north the British and French marched to the aid of the Belgians but were quickly shocked to discover that they were heavily outgunned and outnumbered by the invading Germans. After the initial battles at Charleroi and Mons they had no alternative but to

MAP 1. GENERAL AREA MAP

retreat until they could gather sufficient forces to retake the offensive. For the British, with their small professional Expeditionary Force, this meant the famous and painful 'Retreat from Mons', which lasted from 24 August to 6 September, until the BEF struck back as part of the concerted allied action which became known as the First Battle of the Marne. During most of the Retreat the BEF attempted to stay ahead of the pursuing Germans, and slow them down by blowing bridges and using the Cavalry Division to guard their rear and flanks. By and large the tactic was successful, and the main bodies of marching soldiers, of both sides, stayed out of contact apart from the major rearguard action of the Battle of Le Cateau, which was forced on the British on 26 August. However, on 31 August General von Kluck ordered his *First Army* to make extra efforts to catch the allied forces. As a result on the morning of 1st September the BEF was attacked at three locations. The most significant, although not the largest of these three actions, was at Néry.

During the night of 31 August the German *4th Cavalry Division* penetrated the British Defence Line and arrived on a plain in a gap between two British Corps and just 30 miles from the outskirts of Paris. With its three brigades of cavalry and three batteries of guns it could have wrought havoc among the British logistic units, thereby delaying the retreat and perhaps causing sizeable elements of the BEF to be surrounded and captured by the quickly approaching German *First Army*. Just as the rapid advance of Rommel's armoured division in May 1940 unbalanced the British defence around Arras, General von Garnier's

**The British Expeditionary force in Boulogne. A Horse Artillery Battery moves off after disembarkation**

cavalry division could have caused chaos among the retreating units of the BEF and changed the outcome of the war of movement in 1914. However, von Garnier's scouts spotted a British cavalry brigade bivouacked at Néry "without any obvious defence" and he chose to launch an immediate attack on this vulnerable target.

Thus, early on the first morning of September 1914, the British 1 Cavalry Brigade was surprised in its billets, in the village of Néry, by a greatly superior force of German cavalry and artillery. All the advantages were with the German *4th Cavalry Division*. It outnumbered the British by more than two to one, but within three hours of launching its attack the German division had lost most of its guns and was in rapid retreat, and barely avoided its own complete destruction. This brief action, which was just a small incident in the 'Retreat from Mons', illustrated both the advantages and disadvantages of the modern use of cavalry. The outnumbered British fought back tenaciously on horse and foot making the best use of cover and as a result were able to drive off the German cavalry and, for the first time in the Retreat, the British were left in command of the battlefield. As a result, this short but gory battle has probably been written about more than any other event during the Retreat. It epitomised the British underdog fighting against overwhelming odds, and quickly became famous as an example of the triumph of discipline over adversity, and of the heroism of the horse gunners who, despite being surprised, fought against overwhelming odds until they had fired the last shell from their last surviving gun.

Not only was this action the first during the Retreat when British forces were left in command of the field; it was also the first time that

German guns were captured by the British. The centre of the battle was the heroic stand by the horse gunners who earned three VCs that morning, but this action has many other lessons. Why was the British brigade caught napping? Why in spite of their initial advantages did the Germans fail to break the British, and suffer so badly themselves? Why was the German division so badly mauled that it required three days rest to recover and was never able to take part in the German advance again; indeed from then on it was relegated to flank protection duties. What impact did this short action have on the outcome of the War, particularly the ensuing Battle of the Marne?

This account uses eyewitness accounts from both sides to explain how the British and German formations met at Néry; how the battle developed and how the Germans were forced to abandon their attacks and their guns. Moreover, it follows the fleeing German units after the battle and their attempts to avoid contact with the strong British forces, which were all around them. Finally it attempts to assess the impact of this small but significant action on the ensuing Battle of the Marne.

## ADVICE TO TOURERS

Today Néry is a sleepy dormitory village well off the main roads. There are no accommodation or restaurant facilities in the village, but visitors are always welcome, particularly at the Marie, where there are momentos of L Battery and printed guides to the site of the battle. Access from the Calais-Paris autoroute is from Junction 9, which is marked Creil. After the motorway tollbooth take the D122 just a short distance to the centre of Verberie, where restaurants and hotels may be found.

There are also local hotels and restaurants in Crépy-en-Valois and Villers-Cotterêts. Villers-Cotterêts also has an excellent Ibis hotel in the north of the town, which is not far from the poignant memorial in the forest to the more than a hundred guardsmen who were killed fighting on the morning of 1 September against the attack launched by German *III Corps*.

To reach Néry from the centre of Verberie, follow the D932A up the hill out of the town. After crossing the new TGV bridge, take the first road on the left, the D26 to Raray and Rully. After about a kilometre there is a junction with the D554 road to Néry. This passes the La Borde farm and runs directly to the main crossroad in Néry, opposite the L Battery field, which was the centre of the action that morning.

The battle at Néry was a short action fought during the War of Movement, so there are no battle remains or ground works to indicate where the action was. Néry itself is a very old community, established astride an ancient Roman road, and with many buildings whose foundations go back at least until the Middle Ages. However, as the village is off the beaten track, it has remained practically undisturbed by modern development and its main streets and buildings are still largely much as they were in 1914. Therefore it is easy to see where the action took place, and imagine how vulnerable the men and their horses, stabled in the open, were to German guns firing from the high ground to the east. It is also obvious that those soldiers, who had the good fortune to be billeted within the ancient farms, were easily able to defend the thick stone buildings and remain well protected.

Most of the RHA mortalities were buried in the small communal cemetery in Néry. However, other gunners and many of the cavalry were buried at the Military Cemetery at Verberie and at the communal cemetery at Baron, some ten miles southwest of Néry, which was the site of a field hospital where many of the wounded from Néry were taken immediately after the action.

# ACKNOWLEDGEMENTS.

I wish to acknowledge my gratitude to the following for their help and permission to publish extracts, photographs or maps:

Dr. Anthony Clayton, formerly a lecturer at the Royal Military Academy Sandhurst, who provided guidance and encouragement to proceed with this project.

Mr. David Webb, son of Sergeant Frederick Webb of The Queen's Bays, who provided the photographs and accounts of his father's heroic action at Néry, and who joined me for the ninetieth anniversary of the battle at Néry.

M. Pierre Martinaud, Chairman of the Néry Historical Society who has been unfailingly helpful, conducted me over the battlefield, and joined us for the ninetieth anniversary of the battle at Néry.

Mrs. Brenda Field, daughter of Trooper William Clarke of B Squadron, The Queen's Bays, for permission to use his accounts and photographs.

Mr. William Liversidge son of Trooper Liversidge of B Squadron, The Queen's Bays, who was wounded at Néry and later captured at Baron, for permission to use his photographs.

The Royal United Services Institute and its excellent librarian John Montgomery, who provided ready access to their splendid collection of

11

journals and regimental histories, and for permission to quote from accounts of the battle by Major Lamb, General Pitman and others contained in The Cavalry Journal and the account by Major Becke found in the RUSI Journal.

Mr. Andrew Orgill librarian of the Royal Military Academy Sandhurst Library for access to the General von Kluck's biography and other rare books.

The Curator of the Royal Welch Fusiliers Museum for permission to quote from the remarks of Major Yates RWF contained in "The War the Infantry knew" by Doctor JC Dunn.

The Royal Artillery Historical Trust for permission to quote from the accounts by Captain Burnyeat, and Sergeant Nelson VC as well as from the paper delivered by Lieutenant General the Lord Norrie, to the Royal Artillery Historical Society on 3 November 1967 and to Mr. Paul Evans, Librarian of Firepower, the Royal Artillery Museum, Woolwich for his knowledgeable assistance and help.

Mr.Chris Sheppard, Head of Special Collections at the Liddle Collection at Leeds University Library, the University of Leeds for permission to quote from the account of Colour-Sergeant E M Lyons of the Royal Warwickshire Regiment.

The Library and staff of the Imperial War Museum for access to their collection of German regimental histories.

## LIST OF MAPS

## Chapter One

# THE GERMAN ADVANCE INTO BELGIUM AND FRANCE

The *4th Cavalry Division* crossed the border into Belgium on 4 August 1914. It was one of the three cavalry divisions of General von der Marwitz's *II Cavalry Corps*. Its task, as part of the combined group of cavalry, infantry and artillery led by General Emmich, was to beat a path through the Belgian defences, to prepare for the rapid advance by the right wing of the German Army to the borders of France.

This attack on neutral Belgium by the German army was an essential first step in the Schlieffen Plan, which had been developed by General Alfred von Schlieffen, who became Chief of Staff of the

**The Belgian town of Vise was the first to fall into German hands. Troops are seen searching the ruined buildings, perhaps in expectation of loot.**

German army in 1891. His vision depended on defeating France first, then quickly turning and defeating Russia. The plan aimed to absorb the French attacks in the southern areas of Alsace and Lorraine and then achieve victory by outflanking the strong chain of fortresses on the eastern frontier of France and overcoming the French army in a whirlwind campaign. It contained a very precise timetable, which was designed to enable Germany to mobilise quickly and muster sufficient forces on its western border so that it could concentrate on knocking out France within the first forty two days of a conflict. The Plan accepted the risk of launching seven German armies against the French and placing just one army in the east to defend against the expected Russian attack. A rapid defeat of France, according to the Plan, would then leave Germany free to move the bulk of its forces eastward to deal with the enormous Russian army, which was predicted to need at least forty days for its mobilisation.

The Schlieffen Plan assumed that an overwhelming force could be concentrated on the French and Belgian borders, which would be able to sweep rapidly through Belgium and northern France with the target of besieging and capturing Paris within forty days, or decisively defeating the French field armies. Year by year, the Plan was refined and tested in countless exercises and went hand in hand with a steady increase in the size of German forces. Eventually, in order to position strong German armies in the north of France, which would be strong enough to guarantee victory; the Plan developed from requiring a purely technical infringement of Belgium territory (in 1897) to a full-blooded invasion and destruction of all Belgium's military defences in 1905.

The Plan had two major problems. The first was that von Schlieffen struggled with the logistical problem of getting sufficient forces into northern France to be able to overcome the French field forces and occupy Paris according to his timetable. Additional forces could have been available from a swelling German population, but any additional units would have had to be fitted onto the available roads and supplied by horse transport as they moved further from their bases, and this would in turn slow down the rate of advance and destroy the timetable.

The second integral problem was that the planned route for outflanking the French border fortresses by the three strong armies of the German right wing required the invaders to pass through Belgium and Luxembourg. However, Britain, France and Prussia had guaranteed the neutrality of Belgium on its foundation by their treaty of 1839. In 1898, during a State visit to Germany, the Kaiser had actually asked the old Belgian King, Leopold II, for the right to a free passage through Belgium

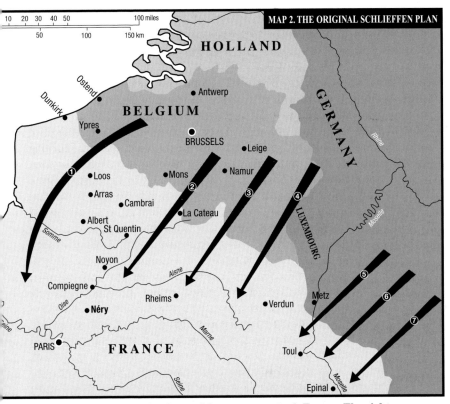

**Seven German armies pivoting on Metz were to attack France. The right wing was particularly strong while the left wing was deliberately set to be weaker and merely hold the French Armies on its front.**

for the German Army, which King Leopold had totally rebuffed. In previous continental conflicts Britain had been the traditional ally of Prussia and Austria against France, but attacking Belgium risked the possibility of involving Britain on the same side as France. This was clearly not seen as much of a risk in 1905, or indeed a risk with very serious consequences. It was impossible for Germany, with its huge and growing army, to predict that it had much to fear from Britain which, while it dominated the world's seas with its huge navy, had only a small army, most of which was based in the Empire. Indeed, the Kaiser, grandson of Queen Victoria and a British (honorary) Field Marshal, simply could not imagine that war with Britain was remotely likely. Moreover, in 1905 the *Entente Cordiale* had only just been concluded between Britain and France, and it took almost ten years to develop this from a sentiment into a plan for serious military co-operation.

Under the Schlieffen Plan, seven strong armies (eighty per cent of the German Army) were created for the task of defeating the opposing five French armies located close to the border with Germany. Von Schlieffen determined that the preponderance of weight of forces would be placed on the northern (right) wing, which would drive through Belgium and northern France and would swing like a door hinged on Metz and Thionville. The Plan envisaged that the left wing German armies would be only just strong enough to contain the opposing French forces. Further, to the extent that the French did the Germans a favour, and committed their major effort on their right, it would deliberately allow the German armies there to wheel back into good defensive territory, absorbing the energy of the attacking French right wing. Thus the beauty of pivoting the armies on Metz and Thionville would mean distracting and absorbing French military energy in good defensive territory, while the decisive force of the German army was driving deep into northern France through open country, where it could defeat the outnumbered French armies and isolate the French capital.

For their part, the French were determined to avenge themselves for the unpalatable defeat of 1871 and had refined their plans to vanquish the Germans. Bizarrely, the French had developed their own war-winning plan, Plan XVII, which precisely involved their driving into the lost provinces to recover them and threaten the Rhine and the rear of the German forces. Thus, execution of Plan XVII would result in the French exactly conforming to the expectations of the German Schlieffen Plan. However, von Schlieffen retired in 1906, and the

**General von Kluck.**

execution of the plan was left to his successor, General von Moltke (nephew of the General and military theorist who had achieved the signal victory over the French in 1870-71). He gradually weakened the balance of the plan by allowing most of the new divisions, which were created by a growing population, to go to the southern armies. He appeared to believe that the Schlieffen Plan could be improved by defeating the

The Kaiser with Moltke (on his right) and staff on horseback, surveying manoeuvres.

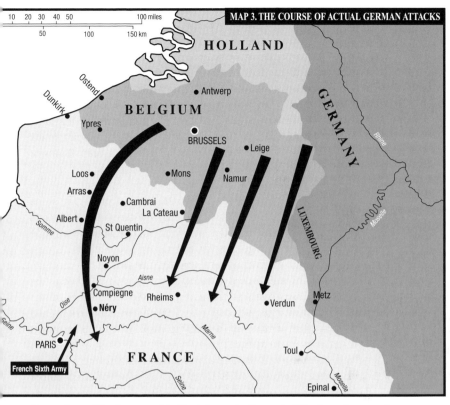

MAP 3. THE COURSE OF ACTUAL GERMAN ATTACKS

**General von Kluck swung his First Army to the east of Paris and exposed his flank to the newly created French Sixth Army from Paris.**

French on both wings and encircling what was left in a Cannae-type operation.

Leading the German forces on the right wing for the advance through Belgium, was a special task force drawn from each of the three armies of the right wing. It was led by General Emmich, whose task was to reduce and occupy the Belgian fortresses quickly. For this role Emmich had been given six infantry brigades and *II Cavalry Corps*. Emmich's

17

force was followed by the *Second Army* under Colonel General von Bülow. who also temporarily commanded the far larger *First Army* under Colonel General von Kluck (which followed in echelon behind *Second Army* until there was room for it to move to the outside of the wheel), and the smaller *Third Army* under Colonel General von Hausen. The strong right wing originally comprised thirty four infantry divisions organised into ten active corps and seven reserve corps, with five divisions of cavalry organised into two corps. However, both before and during the invasion, General von Moltke allowed this overwhelming force to be reduced from the original plan, due to the stiff resistance from the Belgians and the fear induced by Russian advances in the east. Far from sticking to the Schlieffen admonition to keep the right wing strong, von Moltke allowed four corps (almost twenty five per cent of its infantry strength) to be dissipated.

**General von Moltke.**

The German invasion of Belgium began on 4 August. Although the Belgian Army resisted valiantly, and imposed far more delay on the German army than it expected, it was inevitably overwhelmed and forced, despite the outstanding leadership of King Albert, to retreat into the redoubt of Antwerp. The BEF and the French Fifth Army moved up slowly to the border of Belgium to ensure there was no appearance of compromise of Belgian neutrality by the allies before the German invasion and brutal destruction of its cities was clearly revealed to the world. However, French intelligence completely underestimated the size and intentions of the German forces, and when the French and British moved across the border to the Sambre River and Mons Canal in late August, they were still unaware of the huge superiority in numbers possessed by the advancing German forces. The fourteen infantry divisions of the two allies found themselves facing three German armies consisting of twenty six infantry divisions (despite losing eight divisions from the original plan). For this war of rapid movement, the allies also had three cavalry divisions to match against the two German cavalry corps, comprising five divisions of cavalry and ten Jäger battalions. The ten divisions of the French Fifth Army found themselves facing the German *Second Army*, while the four infantry divisions of the British Expeditionary Force (BEF), on the left of Fifth Army, came up against von Kluck's *First Army* of ten divisions and (usually) parts of von der Marwitz's *II Cavalry Corps*.

Faced by such odds, the outnumbered and outflanked British and French armies had little alternative but to retreat to avoid encirclement

and destruction. This was actually managed in relatively good order and both the French and British armies remained intact as they retreated. After imposing a significant delay on the Germans at Mons on 23 and 24 August, the BEF divided into its two separate corps for the retreat south, but managed to stay ahead of the Germans until 26 August. On that day I Corps, under General Haig, was caught at Landrecies but suffered relatively light losses, before getting away. However, at Le Cateau the worn-out troops of the two divisions of II Corps, which had already suffered the brunt of the attacks at Mons, together with those of Major General Snow's newly arriving 4th Division, found themselves forced to stand and fight. These three divisions were heavily attacked by five infantry divisions of *First Army* and by elements of the three divisions of *II Cavalry Corps*. Although they fought back grimly, they were in danger of being overwhelmed near the end of the day, when they were aided by the support of Sordet's Cavalry Corps and French territorials. As a result most of the British units got away just in time and largely managed to stay ahead of the pursuing Germans. Nevertheless, on that day at Le Cateau, General Smith-Dorrien suffered more casualties than Wellington did at Waterloo.

General Haig.

General Smith-Dorrien.

This was just a token harbinger of the losses to follow in later

**German cavalry equipped with lance, sword, pistol and carbine on the march through Belgium.**

battles, but undoubtedly so worried Field Marshal Sir John French that he seriously considered withdrawing the BEF completely from the battlefield. Field Marshal French felt that retreating French forces continually exposed his flanks, and there was a real danger of the small British Army of about 100,000 men being completely encircled and destroyed. Undoubtedly he seriously planned to withdraw beyond Paris, until, on 1 September, at a critical meeting with the Secretary of State for War, Field Marshal Kitchener, in Paris, he was ordered to stay in the line and continue supporting the French. In any event, after Le Cateau, the main aim of the British was to outmarch the Germans and delay their advance by

**Sir John French.**

blowing bridges; while they stayed just ahead of them and tried to reorganise, out of contact.

General Joffre, commanding all the French armies, ordered General Lanrezac and his Fifth Army to relieve the pressure on the British and delay the German *Second Army* by an attack at Guise on 29 and 30 August. Lanrezac delivered an effective and surprising counterattack on the German *Second Army*, which at first requested help from *First Army*, and then later reported a victory. The French had only intended to deliver a stopping blow to delay the Germans, so they withdrew as soon as they had halted the German advance. Nevertheless the French withdrawal allowed von Bülow to claim a victory, and declare a halt on 31 August to rest and reorganise his troops, while Fifth Army escaped across the River Oise.

**General Joffre.**

However, the request for help from von Bülow enabled General von Kluck, commanding the *First Army*, to make a fundamental change to the original Schlieffen Plan. Instead of continuing in a south westerly direction, and encircling Paris, he decided to attempt to shorten the war by marching south east in order to catch the flank of the Fifth Army, and also deal with the annoying BEF, if he could find it. As a result of this change of direction, his advance elements caught up with the British on the morning of 1 September.

# Chapter Two

# 1 CAVALRY BRIGADE MOVES INTO NÉRY

1 Cavalry Brigade was commanded by Brigadier-General Charles J Briggs CB, an extremely experienced cavalry officer, who had taken command of the brigade in Aldershot in 1912. He personally understood the importance of active defence against a strong enemy from his experience of fighting against the Boers. During the Boer War he had commanded the Imperial Light Horse Regiment, a tough, locally-recruited cavalry unit. He had once led the ILH in a successful defence against a surprise attack from a Boer cavalry force of over 400 men. His 175 men fought a rearguard action covering their withdrawal,

**Map 4. The Néry area.**

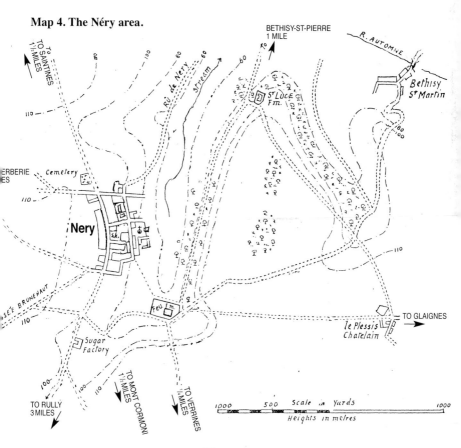

**Brigadier-General Briggs.**

squadron by squadron, for over four miles before they regained their camp, and were able to drive off the Boers with shellfire. This successful fighting withdrawal led, several days later, to the British victory of Wildefontein. As a result of his experiences, Brigadier-General Briggs constantly reminded the units of 1 Cavalry Brigade of the importance of mutual support in billets and maintaining local protection at all times. These lessons would be driven home again during the violent action at Néry on the morning of 1 September, 1914.

1 Cavalry Brigade consisted of a small signals troop and three regiments of cavalry, supported by a Royal Horse Artillery battery of six guns; making a total of about 2,000 men when at full strength (which, due to the engagements in which it had already participated, it was not in September 1914). 1 Cavalry Brigade was one of the four brigades of the British Cavalry Division, which, together with one independent brigade, was the cavalry arm of the BEF. The cavalry were used mainly for reconnaissance, to support rearguards, or to guard flanks and maintain links with neighbouring formations. A British cavalry brigade was less than one half of the size of a German cavalry division, which would, in addition to six cavalry regiments, normally have an artillery battalion with twelve guns and one or two Jäger (Light Infantry) battalions in support.

The British cavalrymen all wore the same khaki uniforms and flat Service Dress caps. Campaigning against the Boers had taught them that this dull uniform was more sensible than the exotic uniforms, brass helmets and breast plates still worn by much of the French cavalry. In addition they enjoyed a major advantage over the German cavalry, which was that they were armed with, and taught to use, the same rifle as the British infantry. Their standard procedure, when required to fire, was to dismount and fire from the kneeling or lying position. Their opponents, the German cavalry, in addition to a lance, sword and a pistol, carried a carbine, which was far less accurate than the British rifle.

Despite their seeming khaki uniformity, each of the regiments in 1 Cavalry Brigade maintained an individual identity linked to their

**The main street in Néry today.**

glorious history and traditions. The 2nd Dragoon Guards (The Queen's Bays) was one of the oldest cavalry regiments in the British army. It had been raised by James II to deal with the Monmouth Rebellion in

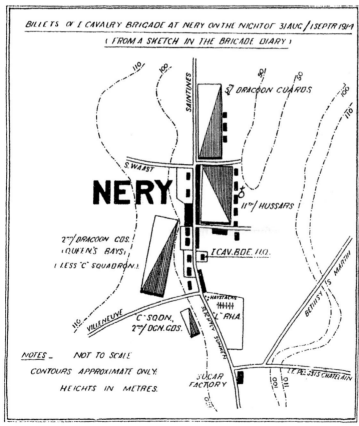

**Map 5. Sketch of the locations of 1 Cavalry Brigade units.**

June 1685. Originally the regiment was named the Queen's Regiment of Horse, to distinguish it from the "Blues", who were already known as the King's Regiment of Horse. It was a matter of pride that all the regiment's horses were bay-coloured. The Queen's Bays had served for much of their history in India and during the Indian Mutiny had won three VCs and taken part in a famous cavalry charge during the Relief of Lucknow in 1858.

The 5th (Princess Charlotte of Wales's) Dragoon Guards were also formed in the turbulent period when James II, the brother of Charles II, was trying to retain his throne. The 5th Dragoon Guards had been raised initially as Shrewsbury's Horse in 1685 by the Duke of Shrewsbury. Dragoons were originally conceived as a type of mounted heavy infantry, who with their weight and mobility could put down swiftly the rebellions of the poor peasants who followed the standard of such claimants to the throne as the Duke of Monmouth (the oldest illegitimate son of Charles II) or deal with the wild Scotsmen who followed the Stuarts. During the Crimean Campaign it had formed part of the Heavy Brigade, which had successfully charged and scattered a seemingly overwhelming force of Russian cavalry on the morning of 25 October 1854 at Balaclava.

The German crown prince.

The 11th Hussars (Prince Albert's Own) was the youngest cavalry regiment in the Brigade; having been raised in Essex in 1715, as Honeywood's Dragoons, in response to the Jacobite Rebellion of that year. It too had been involved in many of the most famous engagements in British military history including the Battle of Waterloo, and the Charge of the Light Brigade at Balaclava on the afternoon of 25 October 1864. The regiment was known as the 11th Light Dragoons until 1840, when it fell under the command of that irascible martinet, the Earl of Cardigan. Due to his efforts and keenness to have the regiment appear very smart, it was chosen to greet the Prince Consort at Dover, and escort him to London for his marriage to Queen Victoria. As a result, Prince Albert agreed to become the Colonel-in-Chief, and the designation of the regiment was changed to the more brilliant 11th, Prince Albert's Own, Hussars. In 1854, the aging Earl of Cardigan was actually to lead the Charge of the Light

Brigade and, although this resulted in the destruction of his three light cavalry regiments, he himself emerged entirely unhurt. A later connection with German royalty was also established in October 1911, when the German Crown Prince was invited to become the Colonel-in-Chief of the 11th Hussars. In fact, just prior to the outbreak of War, he had presented its officers with a new portrait of himself in the ornate dress uniform of the Colonel-in-Chief of the 11th Hussars. The Crown Prince was now leading the attack by two German armies against the central French armies; obviously his appointment as Colonel-in-Chief had lapsed.

The 11th Hussars (known familiarly as the "Cherry Pickers", due to the cherry coloured overalls (trousers) which they wore in their dress uniform) had been stationed in India during the Boer War and had not actually taken part in that conflict. However, parties from the Regiment did participate, and by the war's end over half the Regiment had served in South Africa. It had been part of 1 Cavalry Brigade since it was formed in Aldershot in October 1911, and was commanded by Lieutenant Colonel Thomas (Tommy) Pitman.

The youngest element of the brigade was L Battery, its Royal Horse Artillery battery. The Royal Horse Artillery had not been formed until 1793, but such was their value in providing immediate fire support to the cavalry that for many years they had the right, when on parade with their guns, to march in advance of all other army units, including the Household Cavalry. One RHA battery of six thirteen-pounder horse-drawn guns was attached to each of the cavalry brigades. However for administration, two RHA batteries were organised into a Brigade, which in the case of L Battery, was the VII Horse Artillery Brigade, comprising L and I Batteries and the VII Brigade Ammunition Support Column.

L Battery was commanded by Major the Honourable Walter D Sclater-Booth, who had taken over command in Ireland in 1910. His Battery Captain was Captain Edward Bradbury, who had served with the Imperial Yeomanry in the South African War and with the King's African Rifles before joining the Battery in 1910. The battery of five officers, almost 200 men, and some 228 horses was organised into three sections. Each section had two of the modern 13-pounder QF guns, which had been issued to the RHA in 1905. These Quick Firing guns not only had buffer recoil systems but also were the first to be issued with bullet-proof shields to provide some protection for the gun detachment. Gunner Darbyshire says that when necessary they could fire at the rate of fifteen rounds per minute. Each gun had its own limber containing twenty four rounds of shrapnel shells for immediate use and was accompanied by two ammunition wagons. The battery was a complicated organisation with many specialists (such as farriers and smiths), drivers and gunners to look after the horses, guns and limbers, and supply wagons. The man who actually organised the work of the battery was the Battery Sergeant Major (BSM) George T. Dorrell. Despite his comparative youth (he was only 34 years of age), he was a very experienced soldier, having enlisted in the Royal Artillery in 1895, had served in the Boer War, and had been BSM since 1911.

L Battery had already distinguished itself in a number of actions following the Battle of Mons. On 24 August, during the second day of the Battle of Mons, the Germans attempted to envelop the left wing of the BEF held by the 5th Division, with the *7th and 8th Divisions* of the *German IV Corps*. The Germans launched a mass attack by the twelve battalions of the *8th Division*, from the direction of Quievrain, against the divisional rearguard made up by the Norfolks and Cheshires supported by 119 Battery RFA. This mass infantry attack might have succeeded but for the action of L Battery, which came forward and drove the infantry back by bursting its shrapnel shells low with terrible effect on the masses of German infantry. L Battery held up the German attack for nearly three hours and was instrumental in ensuring that most of 5th Division avoided being surrounded by the Germans. Major Tom Bridges, of the 4th Dragoon Guards, coming back from an unsuccessful charge against the advancing German infantry, saw some of the L Battery guns still firing and holding up the masses of German infantry. He reported seeing:

*two British guns firing away at the advancing German hordes*
*as steadily as if they had been on the range at Okehampton.*

L Battery was also in action again two days later covering the British right flank at the Battle of Le Cateau and, due to casualties in these actions, L Battery was below its full mobilised strength.

During 31 August, the three cavalry brigades of the Cavalry Division (not including 3 Cavalry Brigade, commanded by the wilful Brigadier-General Gough, who had detached his brigade, and was operating with the independent 5th Cavalry Division) had stayed close together as they had waited for signs of enemy cavalry activity, and patrolled to the west of Compiègne. Their orders on 31 August had included guarding the crossings of the River Oise until midday, when the bridges were supposed to have been blown-up by engineers from the 4th Division. Unfortunately the bridges at Bailly and at Compiègne itself were not demolished (because the bridges were just too solid!).

1 Cavalry Brigade had originally received orders to go into billets at

**British cavalry bivouac in Northern France.**

Sarron that evening, but because this was already occupied by French cavalry, it was then directed to the small village of Néry. The Brigade re-crossed the Oise at Verberie and passed through the 4th Division units, which were headquartered at and around Verberie. Finally at about 6 pm it started to move into its Néry billets for the night. The Battery was the last unit to arrive at Néry, having stopped in Verberie to water the horses, as it was thought that the resources at Néry would be too limited to water all the horses of the Brigade before nightfall.

The billeting party, which went ahead of the brigade directly from Venette to Néry, comprised: the Brigade Major, Major JS Cawley; Captain EK Bradbury (second in command of L Battery); and Lieutenant de Labouchere of the French 6th Dragoons (liaison officer with the Queen's Bays). Brigade headquarters was established in the Mairie, and the Staff Captain, Captain Osborne, made detailed accommodation allocations. The 11th Hussars acted as advanced guard for the brigade that day and provided march protection and security picquets for the brigade as its units moved into the village.

The village of Néry was actually in II Corps area, but was given to 1 Cavalry Brigade because no alternative accommodation was available in the newly-formed III Corps area. The new corps had just been formed on 30 August from the 4th Division and the independent 19 Brigade, and was intended to form the left wing of the BEF. Unknown to Brigadier-General Briggs, there was actually a large gap in the general defence line between the outposts of the left-hand division of II Corps at Crépy and 19 Brigade at Saintines, north east of Néry. Brigadier-General Briggs was not informed that this gap existed and assumed that the general outpost line covered the northern approach. In fact 1 Cavalry Brigade was the only major unit in this gap of more than five miles. It was this gap which was exploited by the

27

**The main street of Néry today, looking north.**

German *4th Cavalry Division* as it moved south through the night, and made its unnoticed approach to the high plain east of Néry.

Néry village has almost the shape of a 'D', with an old Roman road running almost due north to south. The rounded side of the 'D' fronts on a steep-sided ravine, which lies to the east of the village and separates it from the escarpment bordering the plateau on the south side of the Automne valley. In parts the base of the ravine is flat and cultivated. In other parts, particularly to the north east of Néry, it is very steep and wooded, with a stream running through it. On the western side of the ravine it slopes fairly steeply down to the bottom but has paths running through it and along it from the village. On the eastern side the escarpment is very steep and virtually impossible to climb or descend. Néry is an ancient village largely built of stone and tile, and at that time had about 600 inhabitants. The natural fortress features of the village has ensured that, over the years, local nobles had built a succession of fortified houses and strongholds, which had now become farm buildings. Almost in the centre of the 'D', on the edge of the ravine, stands the old village church with its high steeple, which can be seen for miles around in almost any direction. To the south of the village was a sugar beet factory with a high brick chimney.

The 5th Dragoon Guards were given the north of the village where they could be accommodated in some of the houses but had to picquet their horses in the open, just across the road from the village cemetery. The 11th Hussars were assigned the two large farm buildings either side of the church on the east of the village and could put most of their horses under cover. The Queen's Bays were billeted in the buildings on the southern side of the village, including the fields south west of the village around the road to Verberie. However, C Squadron was obliged

28

**The square in front of the church pictured in 2006 and above as it looked in 1920.**

to bivouac in the open field south west of the village. L Battery was allocated the large field between the village and the sugar beet factory, with the factory itself as the Battery Headquarters. As units established themselves in the village they took over responsibility for their own local security from the 11th Hussars and established road blocks and billet picquets. Each unit remained responsible for its local security.

L Battery, having watered in Verberie, came in later than the rest of the Brigade and took the time to lay out proper horse lines in the top end of its field. This was the first time this had been done during the retreat and perhaps indicates how secure everyone felt that evening. The field was bounded on the west by the road from Néry to Rully and the south by a small winding lane, which rose to the eastern plain and passed Feu Farm. Coincidentally, Feu Farm had been bought by a German a few years before, but it was empty at this time. On the other side of this lane the land rose sharply towards the sugar beet factory with its high chimney. There is still a factory on the site today, but it

29

now manufactures conveyor belts and there is no chimney. Whilst the battery was busy with its evening tasks, Major Sclater-Booth walked over to the Brigade Headquarters, in the Mairie, to check what protective arrangements had been made for the evening. His orders were to block the two roads which led east and south from the sugar beet factory, and to be ready to move at 4.30am the following morning.

Consideration was given to establishing some kind of outpost on the eastern side of the ravine, but it was considered too difficult to provide support from the village. The brigade, apart from its sentries, then had a peaceful night, until it was roused at 2am to be ready to move off at 4.30am.

**Map 6. Disposition of units on the night of 31 August 1914 as German 4th Cavalry Division approaches 1 Cavalry Brigade asleep in Néry.**

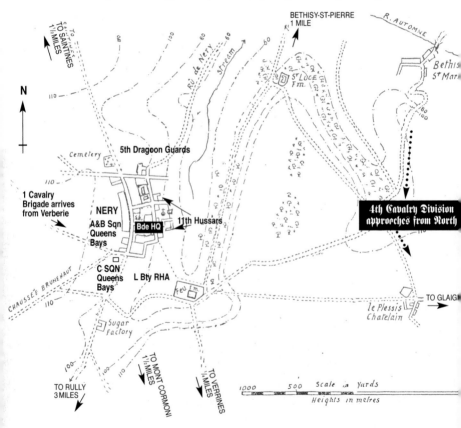

# Chapter Three

## 4th CAVALRY DIVISION OPENS ITS ATTACK

The Germans crossed the Belgian border on 4 August, and despite valiant and stubborn opposition from the Belgian army, which initially delayed them, had finally been able to reduce the main Belgian fortifications and catch up with the Schlieffen Plan timetable. On 21 August the German *Second Army* came up against the French at Charleroi, on the Sambre near the Franco-Belgian border, and on 23 August the German *First Army* met the British at Mons. Given their overwhelming numbers and broad front, the Germans were able to threaten to envelop the allied armies; and to avoid destruction, the British Expeditionary Force (BEF) and the French Fifth Army retreated back into France. The main French field forces consisted of five armies ranged from the Swiss Border to the area north east of Paris. The BEF was the last major formation on the left of the French armies; beyond it were some French territorial divisions covering the open flank. The BEF, consisting initially of just four infantry divisions and one cavalry

**German cavalry watering their horses. Note the Uhlans (Lancers) on the right with their flat topped hats (Tschapka). All German cavalry carried the lance, but of their 93 cavalry regiments only 24 actually were lancers (Ulanen).**

division, was desperately outnumbered and outgunned, and with the French already falling back on its right was forced into a fighting retreat, to avoid being surrounded and destroyed.

Leading the advance of the German *First* and *Second Armies*, were the two cavalry corps of Generals von Richthofen (*I Cavalry Corps*) and von der Marwitz (*II Cavalry Corps*). The cavalry was the pride of the Kaiser's Army and he had deliberately displayed the threatening capabilities of his cavalry on numerous exercises to impress future allies and enemies. By the outbreak of war, Germany could field eleven cavalry divisions, with a total of some 60,000 men, which increased to more than 100,000 by including attached troops. Each division had a basic establishment of 5,200 all ranks, and normally comprised three brigades of cavalry (each with two cavalry regiments divided into four sabre squadrons) and were supported by batteries of horse-drawn field guns and machine guns. In addition, each division had a signals detachment (with heavy and light wireless stations), a pioneer (engineer) detachment, an intelligence detachment, and was accompanied by a large transport column for its supplies. Usually, for operations, each cavalry division would have attached to it one or more Jäger battalions. These were light infantry battalions, comprising four Jäger companies, a cyclist company, and a machine gun company equipped with six machine guns. *I Cavalry Corps* had two cavalry divisions and *II Cavalry Corps* had three cavalry divisions, each corps having a total of five attached Jäger battalions. Riding ahead, or on the flanks of the main armies, these two cavalry corps were switched between the *First* and *Second* Armies as they advanced through Belgium and France.

On 27 August, General von Moltke, Chief of Staff of the German Army, had ordered *First Army* to pass to the west of Paris while *Second Army* was to drive directly for Paris, and the *Third Army* was to pass to the east of Paris. This was confirmation of the classic movement for the encirclement of Paris envisaged in the Schlieffen Plan, but with the enemy armies still largely intact, this still represented a considerable risk to the German forces. Therefore, his order allowed the possibility of abandoning the south westerly direction of advance and instead wheeling to the south, if this became necessary due to enemy opposition.

**General von Moltke.**

After his successes at the Battles of Mons and Le Cateau, General von Kluck felt that he had defeated and driven the small BEF from the field, and that it was then essential to turn and deal with and indeed destroy the major French Armies. He was over-confident. In reality his army at Le Cateau had only met the reinforced II Corps of the BEF. At Le Cateau, II Corps and the 4th Division, supported by the Cavalry Division, had suffered severely, losing some 8,000 men (dead, wounded and missing) and thirty-eight guns, but General Sir Horace Smith-Dorrien had made the best of a bad situation. He had slowed von Kluck's advance and got most of his units away, still in relatively good order. On the right, separated by thick forests, the British I Corps was also

**General von Kluck.**

retreating but still virtually undamaged. On 28 August von Kluck's right wing had defeated General D'Amades's Territorial forces at Péronne and again the following day on the River Avre. These victories eliminated for him any fear that *First Army* would be threatened by the French forces from Amiens in the west, or from Paris. On 28 August, he therefore proposed to General von Bülow, "wheeling inwards" to drive the major French Armies away from Paris.

After a close-fought battle at Guise on the 29 and 30 of August, General von Bülow also mistakenly thought that he had decisively defeated the French Fifth Army, which was the largest of all the French armies. As a result, he believed that the *First* and *Second Armies* had the opportunity to close with and roll-up the entire French line, provided both armies could wheel together and destroy the remnants of the French Fifth Army by a combined frontal and flank attack. Confident of victory after his supposed success at Guise, von Bülow therefore fell in with von Kluck's proposal and formally suggested to him on 30 August that:

> *To gain the full advantages of the victory, a wheel inwards of the First Army pivoted on Chauny towards the line La Fére-Laon is urgently desired.*

This invitation fitted in with von Kluck's own ideas, and he therefore informed von Moltke on 30 August of his decision to change the direction of his advance:

> *The First Army has wheeled round towards the Oise and will advance on the 31st by Compiégne and Noyon to exploit the success of the Second Army.*

In reality, the Battle of Guise had been more of a victory for the French, who had dealt a stopping blow to the Germans, and von Bülow needed to halt on 31 August to rest and reorganise his Army. This day of rest was a desperate necessity for the soldiers of *Second Army*. They were exhausted after their long march through Belgium and France and fighting in the Battle of Guise, and they were actually quite unable to continue the pursuit of the French Fifth Army, which was allowed to break contact and to get away over the River Oise.

However, there was no rest for the footsore soldiers of *First Army*, which was marching on the outside of the great German wheel. General von Kluck, although aged 67, was still full of vitality and had no intention of playing second fiddle to von Bülow. He believed that by extraordinary forced marches he could catch up with the "semi-defeated" French Fifth Army and destroy it by engaging its flank. To exploit the success already achieved, and catch up with the French army, he decided it was essential to march even more quickly and act more boldly. Therefore on 31 August, *First Army*, which was already a day's march ahead of *Second Army*, was ordered to continue marching and attack the enemy aggressively. However, General von Moltke, hundreds of miles away at OHL Headquarters, seemed to think that *First Army* was actually in echelon behind *Second Army*.

General von Kluck ordered General von der Marwitz and his *II Cavalry Corps* to lead the right flank of the advance of *First Army* in the direction of Soissons and Villers-Cotterêts, so that they could pin the left flank of the French Fifth Army. General von Richthofen was ordered to take his *Cavalry Corps* (comprising the *Guard* and *5th Cavalry Divisions*) and lead the left flank of the *First Army* advance and cover the gap with *Second Army*. Von Kluck's intention was to close with the French Fifth Army and to ignore General Maunoury (commanding the defence forces of Paris) or the BEF, unless these forces actually got in the way. So, while *Second Army* took the opportunity to rest and consolidate on 31 August General von Kluck urged his tired soldiers to greater efforts and to increase the speed of their advance.

Leading the right wing of von Kluck's advance was General von der Marwitz and his *II Cavalry Corps*. To reduce the length of columns and give himself more flexibility, he had already divided his corps into four manoeuvre elements. These were his three cavalry divisions (the *2nd*, *4th*, and *9th*), and the five Jäger battalions, which had been withdrawn from the cavalry divisions and formed into a separate *Jäger Brigade*. For the advance on 31 August, General von der Marwitz used the Jägers as a corps flank protection force, covering the approaches to the west of Noyon from Montdidier. During the following night the Jägers were marched and lorried, without any rest, to the south of the

Forest of Compiègne, ready to attack Crépy-en-Valois at dawn on 1 September. Speed of advance was considered essential, and General von der Marwitz ordered his three cavalry divisions to set off very early on the morning of 31 August.

At first General von der Marwitz and his headquarters travelled with *4th Cavalry Division*, which had actually set off at 2am and 3am from Ognolles and Beaulieu (which means they would have got up even earlier). Following them was the *2nd Cavalry Division*. The *4th Cavalry Division* reached the River Oise by 10am and crossed the river at Longueil, southwest of Thurotte, covered by its cyclist detachment. The crossing by a narrow wooden suspension bridge delayed the division, and its commander, General von Garnier, decided to shorten the *4th Cavalry Division* columns by leaving behind the Division's support transport and first-line ammunition supplies. They then passed through the Forest of Laigue, until reaching a rest area at Offémont, on the western side of the Forest. There, at about 4pm, von der Marwitz received reconnaissance reports that there were strong enemy forces in Soissons, Vic, Crépy and Villers-Cotterêts. He therefore decided to change the direction of his Corps' advance to skirt most of these forces and use the cover of the Forest of Compiègne in order to penetrate the enemy outposts with the intention of arriving well south of the Forest by the morning of 1 September. The divisions were ordered to make a noiseless march, in the direction of Nanteuil, as rapidly as possible, and assemble in Rosières early the next morning. They were also ordered to make a 'vigorous offensive in case of enemy resistance.' General von der Marwitz then left with the *2nd Cavalry Division* and headed back in a westerly direction through the forest to Choisy.

Later that night, the German cavalry found that the small town of Verberie, south west of the Forest of Compiègne, was defended by the British 4th Division; and General von der Marwitz ordered the *9th* and *2nd Cavalry Divisions* to undertake night attacks against the British positions. In the event they were too exhausted by their long approach march and felt unable to undertake these risky attacks in the dark without proper reconnaissance, so they bivouacked on the main road in front of Verberie. The night of 31 August was a damp one, and their lack of enthusiasm for a night attack against an unknown enemy, without proper reconnaissance and after a long day in the saddle is understandable. However, it is interesting to compare the lack of enthusiasm of these two tired divisions for launching a night attack with the subsequent boldness of the *4th Cavalry Division*.

Although von Kluck had ordered an advance by *First Army* in a south easterly direction, General von der Marwitz had apparently changed the orders about the general direction of advance for his Cavalry Corps. Instead of heading south east, he was now heading in a south westerly direction towards Nanteuil, which put his cavalry divisions on course to reach the outskirts of Paris within another day's march. In so doing, he thrust his cavalry straight into the middle of the BEF, which was marching due south. Not only had he issued a general order for all his cavalry divisions to attack the enemy wherever they found them, but he had moved the five battalions of Jägers by an overnight march so that they could be in action at dawn on 1 September, attacking the British positions at Crépy-en-Valois.

As it led the *II Cavalry Corps* advance south that day and night, the *4th Cavalry Division* made its way as quickly as possible. The *4th Cavalry Division* had been a key element in the speedy advance by the Germans through Belgium and France. However, resistance by the Belgian army had been more severe than expected. The division had suffered severe losses in Belgium, particularly at Bavemme and then at Haelen on 12 August. Afterwards the division had been placed on the Schelde on 23 August to guard against an imaginary British advance from Ostend, Dunkirk and Calais. *4th Cavalry Division* was also involved in the Battle of Le Cateau at Béthencourt, on 26 August where, together with the *9th Cavalry Division*, they attacked on both sides of the Béthencourt Road, but suffered few casualties.

According to an officer of the *18th Dragoons*, writing after the war, the intention of *II Cavalry Corps* was definitely to reconnoitre towards Paris. The need to make a rapid advance and to reduce any impediment to the speed of the march, led to some more decisions, which were no doubt much regretted later. Some of the led horses, bridging material and telegraph wagons were left behind at the gloomy rest area at Offémont, which undoubtedly reduced the capacity of *4th Cavalry Division* to communicate with the rest of the Army.

Apart from being very tired after an approach march of some twenty-six hours, Lieutenant-General von Garnier's *4th Cavalry Division* suffered from a number of other disadvantages before even beginning its attack at Néry. Theoretically the German cavalry believed in the shock effect of the mounted charge as a decisive battle winner. However, as Colonel JFC Fuller stated in one of his studies in the Cavalry Journal, it was normal for German cavalry units to be well supported in a mounted attack.

> *To provide stability to this curtain of horsemen, Jäger*
> *battalions and Horse Artillery kept close to the heels of the*

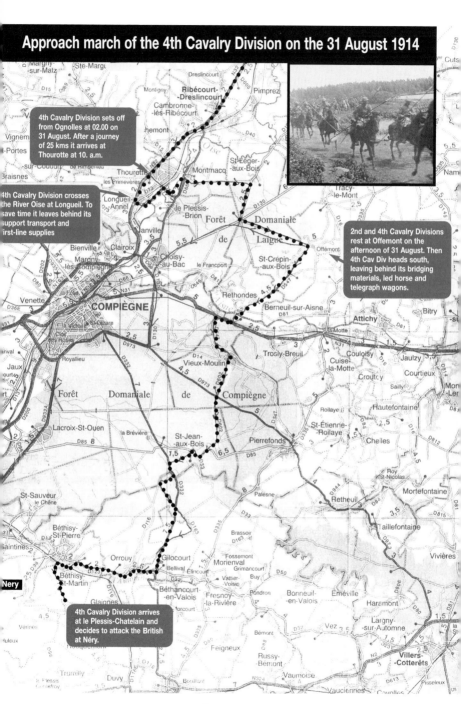

# Approach march of the 4th Cavalry Division on the 31 August 1914

4th Cavalry Division sets off from Ognolles at 02.00 on 31 August. After a journey of 25 kms it arrives at Thourotte at 10. a.m.

4th Cavalry Division crosses the River Oise at Longueil. To save time it leaves behind its support transport and first-line supplies

2nd and 4th Cavalry Divisions rest at Offemont on the afternoon of 31 August. Then 4th Cav Div heads south, leaving behind its bridging materials, led horse and telegraph wagons.

4th Cavalry Division arrives at le Plessis-Chatelain and decides to attack the British at Néry.

37

**Belgian Lancers bivouacked after victory at Haelen.**

*troopers who, although their mobility reduced, reaped numerous advantages from this support.*

Colonel Fuller also quoted from an article by Lieutenant-Colonel Poudret in the 1917 issue of the Revue Militaire Suisse, to illustrate the tactical use of support troops by the German cavalry.

*In the fights for villages, the Jäger battalions were generally placed in front, dismounted squadrons on the flanks, and mounted detachments sent by wide turning movements to outflank or occupy the rear exits, thus cutting off the enemy's retreat. This manoeuvre, which was repeated in almost every case, enabled the German cavalry to take a large number of prisoners. Machine guns and cyclists generally accompanied the advanced guards; and cyclists were also frequently allotted to patrols.*

Had they been available, Jägers would have been used for the attack at Néry. Cycle units were used by all sides in the fluid opening actions of 1914, and with their capacity for mobility and silent movement proved their worth time and time again. For example, the *4th* and *2nd Cavalry Divisions* had already suffered severely at the hands of a gallant Belgian unit of 450 cyclists, which was part of the small Belgian Cavalry Division, which defended Haelen on August 12 1914. In particular *17 Cavalry Brigade* (which comprised the *17th & 18th Dragoons Regiments*) of *4th Cavalry Division* suffered severely as it attempted mounted charges against the Belgian cyclists. The *18th*

*Dragoons*, made repeated squadron charges against the Belgian cyclists and as a result had 140 officers and men killed, wounded or captured in this battle. These casualties included the Commanding Officer, Major Baron Digeon von Monteton and his Adjutant, who were both killed in charges. As a result Captain von Anderten from the *17th Dragoons* had taken over command of the *18th Dragoons*. The *17th Dragoons* itself also lost some eight officers, 159 men and 165 horses at Haelen.

*3 Cavalry Brigade* (comprising the *2nd Cuirassiers* and the *9th Uhlans*), which was also heavily involved in the Battle of Haelen, suffered casualties of ten officers, 171 men and some 500 horses. Although only a small proportion of those casualties were actually killed (the *9th Uhlans*, according to their regimental history, only listed fourteen men killed during August), these casualties would have reduced the combat strength of the *4th Cavalry Division* significantly. These losses probably meant that by the end of August it comprised only around 3,000 cavalrymen. *4th Cavalry Division* was also involved in the battle at Le Cateau, on 26 August, but suffered relatively few casualties, although Major Wagner, commanding its horse artillery, was killed and replaced by Captain Winckler.

Lieutenant-General Max von Poseck, who served as the Chief Staff Officer of *I Cavalry Corps* and later became the German Army's Inspector of Cavalry, states that these actions in Belgium taught the German cavalry bitter lessons about the futility of mounted attacks against good defensive positions. He reported that while the cavalrymen were prepared to attack without regard for casualties,

> '*on the other hand, this day taught that these modern fire positions could not be successfully attacked by mounted troops and, in such a case, only a fire action would be successful.*'

The British, with their hard-won experience from South Africa, had already learnt the value of ensuring their cavalry were trained to fire accurately from dismounted positions, and this was now their standard procedure. The failure of the action at Néry would underline the futility of cavalry charging sound defensive positions manned by well-trained infantry (or cavalry) with modern rifles and machine guns. It would also reconfirm to the Germans the value of having supporting infantry integrated with the cavalry.

While Lieutenant-General von Garnier did have a small cyclist detachment, which he had used, for example, to protect his crossing of the River Automne at Bethisy St. Martin, he did not have with him the *7th Jäger Battalion*, which usually accompanied his division. This meant that not only did he not have the benefit of their much larger cycle detachment; he particularly did not have their six machine guns. The *7th Jäger Battalion* would, on 1 September, have comprised close to 800 well-trained infantry (having left behind a company in Belgium). Unfortunately for von Garnier, the *7th Jäger Battalion* had already been taken from him to form part of an ad hoc *Corps Jäger Brigade*. The *7th Jäger Battalion* was in fact to be involved in fighting on the same day as *4th Cavalry Division*, as it took part in the attack by leading elements of *IV Corps* against the British rearguard at Crépy-en-Valois.

Von Garnier was obeying General von Kluck's order to keep the enemy unbalanced by advancing boldly with his division through the British lines, on almost a 'Reconnaissance in Force'. However, the decision to sacrifice support for speed had its consequences. The division was required to operate not only without the support of its *Jägers*, but also, due to his decisions, without much of its logistics, including support transport, first-line ammunition supplies, some of the led horses, bridging material and telegraph wagons. As a result, many of the men that he was leading deep into enemy territory, would find that not only would they and their horses have nothing to eat or drink for days, but they would also be without ammunition to defend themselves, and would have no alternative but to conceal themselves deep in the forest to avoid destruction by the enemy.

Speedy advances, which keep the enemy off-balance, often achieve remarkable results in war. However it is worth noting that the strategic effect of all these extraordinary efforts using forced marches etc. was nullified by the fact that the soldiers and their horses became even more exhausted, and took longer to deal with and recover from the opposition which the Germans met from British units on 1 September at Crépy, Villers-Cotterêts and Néry. Moreover, the attacks by *2nd Cavalry Division* at Saintines and *9th Cavalry Division* against the British 4th Division at Verberie hardly merit mention, despite the fact that most of the 4th Division was otherwise involved in the mopping up at Néry. Therefore, despite von Kluck's desire to accelerate the rate of advance, the actual achieved advance of *First Army* on 1 September was less than ten miles, and did not strike the BEF or French Fifth Army to any purpose on that day. Although *First Army* continued its advance on the morning of 2 September, attempting to outflank and surround the British, it missed them (because they had marched away in the night), so little was achieved on that day. Those two days wasted by *First Army* trying to attack and surround the BEF, allowed the

**German cavalry resting during the march through Belgium.**

French Fifth Army valuable time to continue its own retreat and evade contact with the Germans.

*4th Cavalry Division* rode all through the heat of the day of 31 August and the following damp night without a stop for food or rest (apart from just two hours at Offémont). Lieutenant-General von Garnier had lost contact with *II Cavalry Corps Headquarters* when passing through Gilocourt, but he would have known that by his unremitting effort he had crossed through the enemy front line. Von Garnier relied upon his net of far-flung patrols to warn him of the presence of enemy formations. However, he could not hope to remain undetected forever. During darkness his forces had ridden through villages apparently manned by British troops, who had not stopped them. At last the division arrived at Bethisy St. Martin, where the locals at first welcomed them warmly, until they realised that they were greeting not British but German troops! A local farmer, seeing their advance, took the trouble to ride to the British II Corps HQ at Crépy and reported large German forces moving through Bethisy St. Martin. Unfortunately this information was not passed to 1 Cavalry Brigade, innocently sleeping in its billets just a few miles away.

As *4th Cavalry Division* crossed the narrow stone bridge over the river at Bethisy St. Martin, a blocking patrol was established a little to the north at Bethisy St. Pierre. In the village the division had captured three British supply vehicles with their crews. As a result, one of the prisoners, a British officer, was later able to witness the whole attack on Néry from the German gun positions; he was subsequently freed after the action. The division then crossed the railway line and climbed up the long narrow steep hill to the next habitation at Le Plessis-Chatelain, where it rested.

Le Plessis-Chatelain is an isolated collection of strongly fortified stone manor houses and farm buildings, which date from about 1280. It has high walls of stone, heavy wooden gates, barns, manor buildings and even a fortified chapel. There is a local legend that after the battle, some German bodies were thrown into its old well, which remains sealed. In any event, due to its size and commanding position on an otherwise empty plain, it made an ideal location for use as Divisional Headquarters. From Le Plessis-Chatelain it is possible to see the

**Le Plessis Chatelain. This was the German Divisional HQ during the battle and was where many prisoners were captured after the battle.**

church spire of Néry to the west.

Von Garnier must have had plenty to consider early that morning at Le Plessis-Chatelain. His division had been in the saddle for more than twenty-four hours and badly needed rest. While he had successfully crossed through the British lines, the plain on which his troops rested was bare of cover and protection. He desperately needed either to rendezvous with the rest of *II Cavalry Corps* at Rosières; or to hide and rest his division in a good defensive position (ideally a thick wood) prior to continuing his reconnaissance towards the outskirts of Paris (perhaps just another night's march away). Therefore, as he gathered his brigades at Le Plessis-Chatelain, he must have been overjoyed to hear that one of the *17th Dragoons'* patrols, had found a large British unit in the nearby village of Nèry, apparently without any protection or sign of defensive positions.

Lieutenant-General von Garnier decided to exploit the vulnerability of the British position before it changed. Further reconnaissance would perhaps have been wise, although difficult in the morning mist, but this would have taken time. It might also have alerted the British and caused them to hurry off or perhaps to attack him. Already he may have had a report of the 11th Hussars' patrol which had bumped his troops on the plain east of Néry. Furthermore, he could expect the French locals in the villages through which his division had passed to inform the British of his progress. Although he knew that he had limited ammunition stocks with his units, he expected the other two cavalry divisions to be abreast of him as they also headed towards Rosières, and likely to be able to support him, if necessary. All in all he was presented with the juiciest of targets, and in view of the orders he had received for *'as noiseless an advance as possible and a most vigorous offensive in case of enemy resistance'*, it would have been negligent to fail to attack such an attractive, vulnerable target.

Therefore, at about 5am English time, General von Garnier ordered an immediate mounted attack. Apparently without any further detailed reconnaissance, he left it to his sub-commanders to make their dispositions as necessary. He did send an officer's patrol towards Rosières (under Leutnant von Unger of the *18th Dragoons*), perhaps in anticipation of receiving some support from the rest of the cavalry corps. He had lost communication with his corps headquarters hours earlier, and clearly did not know that the other two divisions were, at that moment, stopped and resting on the main road well north of Verberie, at least five to ten miles north west of his position.

General von Garnier's plan seems to have been very simple, and

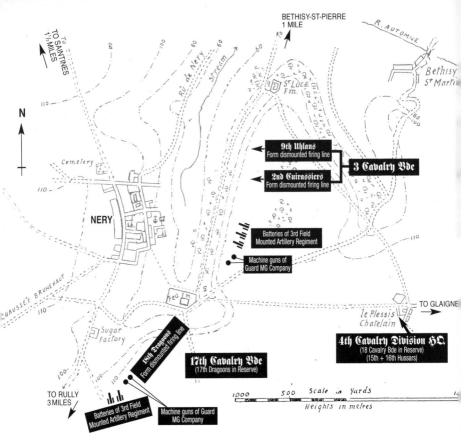

**Map 8. 4th Cavalry Division opens its attack. Early morning 1 September 1914. 4th Cavalry Division begins its attack on Néry with 3 Cavalry Brigade attacking from the North East and 17 Cavalry Brigade fron the South East.**

designed to surprise and destroy the British forces with overwhelming shellfire on the village and mounted flanking attacks. *3 Brigade* (consisting of the *2nd Cuirassiers* and *9th Uhlans*) was to attack on the right, in the area directly east of Néry. From that position it would be able to launch a direct attack on the eastern side of the village or a flanking attack on the north of Néry. It was to be supported by a detachment of the *Guard Machine Gun Company*, and a battery of four guns (or perhaps initially two batteries) of the *3rd Mounted Artillery Battalion*.

*17 Brigade* (comprising the *17th* and *18th Mecklenburg Dragoons)* was placed on the left, on the heights south east of Néry. It was also to be supported by a detachment of the *Guard Machine Gun Company* with two or three machine guns and the remaining one or two batteries of the *3rd Mounted Artillery Battalion*. The *18th Dragoons* were to

View of the long winding hill up from Bethisy St Martin used by 4th Cavalry Division on the night of 31 August as it approached Néry from the North.

make a mounted attack, but the *17th Dragoons* were to be kept in reserve at Le Plessis-Chatelain, and possibly to protect the open southern flank. *18 Brigade* (the *15th* and *16th Hussars*) was also kept in reserve with Divisional HQ at Le Plessis-Chatelain.

These are the dispositions as described by General Max von Poseck in his account of the battle, but may in fact reflect the positions pertaining during the final stages of the battle. Some accounts state that all twelve of the German guns were placed on the ridge east of Néry. Another account by the 11th Hussars (who were directly opposite the eastern ridge) has two batteries of guns placed there, which then moved to the second German gun position, south east of the L Battery field. Apparently the ammunition wagons for these batteries did not move off straight away, but remained on the ridge for some time. This eastern firing position was quite close to the village and vulnerable to return fire, particularly from the machine guns of the 11th Hussars around Néry church and possibly the fire of the 5th Dragoon Guards. The faulty placing of the artillery is mentioned in Lieutenant Colonel von Zieten's report, quoted in the Poseck account;

> *as a consequence of the heavy fog the artillery had approached the enemy too closely and were much troubled by the infantry fire of the English reserves.*

The German artillery had a fairly sophisticated fire control system, but would have suffered from a number of problems in directing their fire. The main problem was the poor visibility caused by the dense morning mist. Also, from either of their fire positions, they would have seen very little of the effect of their fire, apart from in the south of Néry, where the L Battery field was clearly reduced to a shambles very quickly. They may also have seen evidence of the horse casualties caused to the Queen's Bays in the fields around the southern crossroads. However, the machine gun and rifle fire from the 11th Hussars in the stout buildings opposite the eastern ridge, and from the Queen's Bays on the road lining the L Battery field, was clearly effective in stopping the mounted attacks and caused many casualties amongst both cavalry troopers and gun crews.

However, the major source of resistance must have appeared to be the return fire from the guns of L Battery. Therefore it would have been natural to mass the German guns where they could avoid the British machine gun fire and yet be most effective against L Battery's resistance and support the attack on the southern side of Néry, where the main German cavalry attacks were mounted. Sergeant Nelson reports that when Lieutenant Campbell brought the D gun into action behind him, it was able to fire on a squadron of German cavalry, which appeared on the left, and to disperse them. This squadron may have been part of an initial attack by the *18th Dragoons* or by one of the Hussar squadrons, before the futility of mounted attacks against the well-protected British positions was apparent to the German cavalry.

Another explanation is that perhaps not all the guns were unlimbered and in firing positions right from the start of the action. L Battery in its diary reports that two guns were seen in position initially on the crest south east of Néry and that two batteries were on the crest east of Néry. However, other accounts from, for example, Lieutenant de Labouchere, says that three batteries with twelve guns were in action on the ridge south east of Néry almost from the start of the action. He wrote that when he ran down to the L Battery field he could not at first,

> ...*see where the firing was coming from owing to the fog, which was very thick. However, after a few moments he could see the flashes of the German guns to the South-south-east. ...The flashes of discharge from the German guns were now easily seen between Feu Farm and Mont Cormont...at a range of 800 metres.*

This range is corrected in his text to about 500 metres (by agreement with Major Lamb, who translated the article).

The 11th Hussars also reported that the gun battery opposite them moved position to join up with the other guns. Lieutenant Colonel (later Major-General) Pitman, who commanded the 11th Hussars, says in his account of the battle, that three batteries with twelve guns were in line just 400 yards (later measured) from the L Battery position. In his sketch of the battle, all the guns are shown in line, almost due south

46

of Feu Farm, and south east of the sugar factory. Lieutenant (later Lord) Norrie, who led his troop in the final cavalry charge to clear the German guns described the German gun position;

> *One Battery of four guns may have been in position North of Feu Farm, but certainly the other two and, personally, I think, all three, were South East of Néry and Feu Farm.*

In a letter to Soldier Magazine, Lord Norrie wrote that the charge he led from Feu Farm was over the open field;

> *the charge was a spectacular one over 300 yards of open country.*

An interesting account of the start of the battle by Major Yates quoted in 'The War the Infantry Knew', also suggests that the Germans did not immediately launch a co-ordinated attack. He was with the 19 Brigade transport moving off early ahead of 19 Brigade and just passing south through Néry as the attack commenced, with German machine guns opening up on the L Battery gunners, who were washing themselves. According to Major Yates, the German artillery did not open up until later.

> *A lot of the gunners were washing, some had on only their shirts. Suddenly some German machine-guns opened on them from the height on our left. They ran, everyone ran: all our Brigade Transport ran along the road to get clear of the action, and we ran with the rest. I heard afterwards that German artillery came up too.*

Many of the accounts of the battle have different times for the start of the action; varying from 5.05 to 5.50am, and this difference may be due to different parts of the German attack beginning at different times around the village. Lord Norrie stated that he actually looked at his wristwatch at 5.40am when the first shells began landing. In any event, the attack by *4th Cavalry Division* achieved almost complete surprise; beginning with a hail of machine gun fire and shells on the village which struck primarily the horses, men and guns standing in the open in the fields south of Néry, just before 6am.

**German artillery battery preparing to fire.**

# Chapter Four

# THE 11TH HUSSARS RAISE THE ALARM

The 11th Hussars were particularly fortunate in their billeting, being allocated roomy accommodation in two large farms located either side of the prominent church on the east side of Néry. The ground falls away sharply from the church and the two farms, into a pleasant wooded valley, which runs north to south, becoming deeper at the northern end and with a steep escarpment on its eastern side. A stream runs through the valley, and was used by the women of the village who would walk down into the valley to wash their clothes there. Consequently, there were a number of paths running down from the village into the valley. A number of stout stonewalls running along the sides of the hill protected the farms. The 11th Hussars arrived in the village comparatively early (at about 6pm) and it appears some of them were able to make a short reconnaissance that evening of the steep valley on the east side of Néry and of the ridge opposite the village. It was decided not to attempt to man the eastern ridge but, in any event, they set up their two machine guns around the church covering the eastern approach.

The 11th Hussars were responsible for their own immediate area protection during the night and were then, like the other cavalry regiments, supposed to send out an early morning patrol to secure the area to the east of Néry. Captain Halliday, commanding B Squadron, gave instructions to Second-Lieutenant George Tailby to lead this patrol. Major Anderson, Second-in-Command of the 11th Hussars, woke up that morning with 'a curious feeling that something was going to happen' and went to see Second Lieutenant Tailby before he took his patrol out at about 4.15am. In giving this responsibility to a young, inexperienced officer, it is quite clear that no one expected Second Lieutenant Tailby to find anything on his patrol. Fortunately he left his own account of his adventure as he took out his first real military patrol:

> *At dawn on the morning of September 1st I started out with my patrol, which consisted of a Corporal and five men. It was the first patrol I had been sent out on, so I had taken care the night before to select the best men I had in the troop. It consisted of Corporal Parker, one of the pluckiest and most enterprising corporals in B Squadron, and Privates Minton, Dew,*

The farm to the right of Nery Church defended by the 11th Hussars.

Above: The farm as it was in the 1920s, and (below) in 2006.

*Honeybone, Bowler and McCabe.*

*The orders I was given by my squadron leader, Captain Halliday, were to reconnoitre the high ground to the east and south-east of the village, to see if I could observe any hostile movement to the north and to get back as quickly as possible, as units were expected to march soon after dawn. My squadron leader also added that I should probably run into some French picquets, who were reported to be in the neighbourhood.*

*There was thick fog and we could barely see for a hundred yards. I took the quickest route out of the village towards the plateau, and leaving the main road, struck off in a north-easterly direction down a track in the direction of the ridge, crossed the little brook and almost immediately found the steep slopes of the plateau facing me. It was too steep to ride straight up and I found it necessary to take a zig-zag course, along a sheep run, to get up. When on the top I found the fog as dense as ever and decided to look round the edge of the plateau, going to the south end first and then by the edge on to the north and eastern sides. In this way I looked right round the plateau without seeing or hearing anything and had almost come to the spot where I had climbed up, when, through a slight lifting in the fog I perceived at about 150 yards distance to the east, a column of Cavalry. By the appearance of their long cloaks and spiked helmets, I knew they could be none other than the much-heard-of Uhlans. They did not see us, however, for they were dismounted in sections, and appeared to have lost their bearings. They were gazing across the country to the east. They must have just climbed the eastern slope of the plateau, and at the point at which they stood could not have been much more than a mile, as the crow flies, from Néry. At this moment one of my advanced scouts got off his horse and fired at the enemy's advanced point (he told me afterwards he had not seen the main body). That settled it, an order was given and I saw the Uhlans mounting. I shouted out, 'Files about. Gallop'. Now unfortunately I could not get back into the same track that I had come up by, as the head of the German column, now their left flank as they charged towards me, would have cut me off, so I had to gallop towards the edge of the plateau in a north-easterly direction. As luck would have it I just managed to strike off another cart track off the plateau, and gave the order to gallop down it, when suddenly my horse put his foot in a hole, and came down with me at full gallop. I tried to kick him up, but he refused to move, and as by this time the Uhlans could not have been more than fifty yards behind, I shouted to Corporal Parker to take the patrol on and report at once, whilst I plunged into the thicket, which luckily lined the edge of the plateau at this point, expecting at any moment to hear the Uhlans dismount and come after me. Much to my surprise, however, on looking back through the trees, I saw them wheeling round and retiring whence they came. The next thing I saw was Corporal Parker coming up the track and leading my horse, which had apparently got up and followed the patrol down the road. We galloped down the hill, at the bottom of which was an estaminet, outside which was a German cloak and a rifle. A woman said that three Germans had just run out of her house. No doubt they heard us gallop down the hill and went off in a hurry. Enquiring of the woman the direction of the Néry-Bethisy main road, I gave the order to pick up the cloak and galloped on. Before long I struck the main Néry-Bethisy road, close to the level crossing over the railway and, turning to the left, went on in the direction of Néry, which we soon reached.*

*I met no one on entering the village, and sent Corporal Parker to warn the 5th Dragoon Guards, who were at our end of the village, while I rode on towards my squadron, and to report to Regimental Headquarters. Colonel Pitman came out to hear my report, and within an incredibly short space of time, the first shot had been fired.*

Second-Lieutenant Tailby returned at about 5.30am and made his report to his Commanding Officer. At first his report was not believed (by Lieutenant Colonel Tommy Pitman). There were frequent reports of 'Uhlans in the woods' at this time and Uhlans (German Lancers) actually had flat tops on their helmets (tschapka) not spikes, so his patrol had probably bumped into some Cuirassiers, but Tailby was able to produce the German cloak and substantiate his story. As soon as Lieutenant Colonel Pitman had received the report he hurried off to Brigade Headquarters to give warning, while Major Anderson ran down to the 11th Hussars to get the men into their 'stand to' positions. Hardly had Lieutenant Colonel Pitman explained the situation then the first artillery shells began to land. One landed in the Brigade Headquarters where Brigadier-General Briggs was able to pick it up and confirm that it was a German shell. (It seems Brigadier-General Briggs must have been extremely cool to have been able to pick up hot shell fragments and examine them!) With him was Major Sclater-

Booth, who immediately ran back towards L Battery's position.

The 11th Hussars were particularly fortunate that they were in strong stone buildings and, due to the lie of the land, most of the shells and bullets passed over them. In any case, they had been warned about the presence of enemy forces sufficiently early by their own patrol and were prepared for a possible meeting with the enemy. Major Anderson quickly organised the defence of the eastern flank with B and C Squadrons. According to Frederic Coleman, an American who had volunteered to act as a civilian driver with BEF Headquarters and who quoted an officer from the 11th Hussars, the defence of the 11th Hussars area was already organised before the attack began:

*At 5.30 a.m. Lieut Tailby galloped in carrying a German cloak, and reported that his patrol had ridden in the mist right up to a regiment of German cavalry on the ridge north-east of Néry, and had been chased back as far as the ravine.*

*The squadrons were immediately placed into position, B Squadron sending one troop to the south-east corner of the village, one troop to the church overlooking the ravine to the east, one troop to the north-east corner of the village, and one troop being kept in support. C Squadron defended the farm immediately to the South of the church, and A squadron was kept in reserve.*

*Scarcely had these dispositions been made when an extremely heavy artillery and machine-gun fire was opened from the ridge to the north-east of the church.*

Warned by their own patrol, the 11th Hussars were able to respond effectively to the eastern attack, and suffered very few casualties throughout the action. C Squadron occupied the large farm to the south of the church and the B Squadron troops were split up to cover the approaches to the village from the ravine in the southeast and north-east corners and from the farm north of the church. As soon as the defence of the east of the village was organised, Lieutenant Colonel Pitman sent A Squadron to Brigadier-General Briggs to act as Brigade reserve. Briggs used A Squadron to build a barricade at the southern end of the village and to reinforce the Queen's Bays' firing line in the vicinity of L Battery, on the right of B Squadron. Back at the two farms the men and horses had been hardly touched by the enemy fire and they were able to pen up the horses (still saddled) in the small gardens behind some of the houses, which left them free to man the defences. The troopers loop-holed the stonewalls of the two stoutly built farms on either side of the church and returned fire to the

**British infantry dismantling a machine gun.**

enemy positions on the ridge opposite the village.

The 11th Hussars machine gun troop was commanded by Second Lieutenant Dermott McMorrough Kavanagh. At first his two machine guns were placed around the church where they were able to engage the German *3 Brigade* on the other side of the ravine at about 950 yards, which eventually came down to 600 yards. Apparently the initial fire from the eastern ridge was mainly machine gun fire, which seems to indicate either that there was no gun battery there, or that it took a little time for the battery to come into action. The enemy firing from the ridge were clearly dismounted, and the 11th Hussars were amazed to see a complete mounted squadron come into view fleetingly through the mist. Second Lieutenant Kavanagh was just about to order his machine guns to open fire on this wonderful target, when one of the French interpreters begged him not to fire, as he was certain that they were French Cuirassiers. The hesitation allowed the squadron time to move off southwards into the mist and a good opportunity was lost. It seems this could have been a mounted squadron of the *2nd Cuirassiers*, who were operating on this flank, or just possibly it could have been the lead squadron of the *16th Hussars,* led by Lieutenant Colonel Ludendorf, which had, in the fog, blundered close to the ravine as part of its attack against the British forces at the southern end of Néry.

**German wounded at a dressing station.**

Kavanagh, who later commanded the regiment from 1932-36, and eventually served as Crown Equerry to King George VI, always regretted the lost opportunity to use his guns on such a fine target.

Partly due to the mounted action by the 5th Dragoon Guards and the soundness of the defence by the 11th Hussars, the attack by the German *3 Brigade* was totally unsuccessful and they suffered many casualties. Later it became apparent that the dismounted cavalry and guns opposite the 11th Hussars were withdrawn or had moved further south. As a result Kavanagh moved his two machine guns to the south-east corner of the farm buildings, from where they were able to support the Queen's Bays machine gun troop with cross fire, and sweep up and down the main German artillery position. This change of location by the 11th Hussars' machine guns effectively doubled the amount of machine gun fire that could be brought to bear on the German guns. By this time the Germans seemed to have grouped all three of their batteries with their twelve guns together on the south east position near the sugar factory. Whenever the mist cleared enough to see, this cross fire is said by Lieutenant Colonel Pitmen to have been effective and sent many of the gunners running for cover.

By this later stage of the action, the massing of the batteries on the south-eastern firing position and perhaps the appearance of parts of the *Hussar Brigade* south of Néry seems to have indicated that there would be an envelopment attack on this flank. Brigadier-General Briggs therefore ordered that a part of C Squadron of the 5th Dragoon Guards should also be brought down to support the Queen's Bays and A Squadron of the 11th Hussars on the south side of Néry.

Lieutenant Arkwright was in A Squadron 11th Hussars, which was used as the brigade reserve. He kept a diary of the events that day, part of which is quoted below. As usual, his timings do not agree with any others:

> *We get orders to be ready to move off at 4a.m., but at 4 get orders to off-saddle again. At 4.45 we get orders to saddle up at once, as the Germans are close to, and we start to do so with just normal speed, as such orders come at frequent intervals. When we are half ready, when I myself am brushing my teeth at the pump, the Germans get to work with guns, maxims and rifles, at ranges varying from 200 to 1,000 yards. We, the regiment, are lucky in being practically under cover, and all ranks behave as if nothing unusual was happening. We finished saddling up, shut our horses into small yards and 'A' Squadron is set to work to barricade one of the principal entrances to the village; which done we join in the fray outside.*
>
> *I ran outside with my troop behind me and threw myself down in a gap on the bank by the side of the road. Looking about me I saw Cawley (brigade major) on one side of me with a ghastly wound in his head, obviously done for, poor chap, though he was still alive then. On the other side was a gunner corporal firing away with a rifle quite regardless of bullets all about him, and cursing the Germans all the time, saying they had wiped out his battery and he prayed they might all be killed themselves and so on. Just to my right, in a stubble field, was the wreckage of 'L' Battery and a fearful sight it was too. Guns lying all anyhow, a few men crawling about and bunches of them behind two corn stacks in the field. They got one gun out of the field, and the battery sergeant-major and a French officer attached to the Bays kept on with this at intervals for some time. Lining the bank were my troop, about six of the Bays and their maxim gun, which did great work. Opposite we could see 5 German guns 800 yards\* off, but 'L' Battery had silenced three of them before they*

*themselves were snuffed out, and the last gun plus the maxim gradually silenced the others. Things seem to have gone on much the same on the other sides of the village, and eventually they retired after making one last effort to manhandle their guns away. Some time before this I had secured myself a rifle and plugged away into this manoeuvre with a will.*

(*Colonel Pitman's account confirms the distance from this point, since measured, at 450 yards)

It is quite clear that the 11th Hussars were really fortunate in finding themselves in such well-protected accommodation when the attack on Néry commenced. They also received early warning, as a result of which they could prepare for an attack. Not only were their billets in strong well-protected buildings, they were away from the main weight of enemy fire. Moreover, their horses were protected and they were able to mount a squadron to clear up the battlefield at the end of the action. As a result they suffered virtually no casualties to men or horses (only two men and two horses were slightly wounded) and had the ultimate satisfaction of taking control of the battlefield from the enemy and capturing numerous prisoners as well as the first German guns to be captured in the War.

Pitman went on to command 4 Cavalry Brigade from May 1915 and as Major-General T. T. Pitman CB, CMG, he commanded the 2nd Cavalry Division from 1918 to 1919. In 1926 he became Colonel of the 11th Hussars. On his retirement Pitman planted an orchard of apple trees in the formation of a squadron of 11th Hussars. He was such an enthusiastic 11th Hussar that he ensured that all the flowers grown in his garden were either red or yellow, the regimental colours.

# Chapter Five

## THE DESTRUCTION OF L BATTERY IN THE HAY FIELD

L Battery had arrived late in the evening at the hay field just south of the village of Néry, having stopped in Verberie to water the horses as it was thought that the resources at Néry would be too limited to water all the horses of the cavalry brigade. The Battery arrived at about 8pm and found that there was enough space on its bivouac ground to lay out the guns in sections, as per the drill book, and for the horses to be unharnessed for the first time in a week.

The sugar beet factory consisted of a large number of industrial buildings and also some houses, with French civilians still living in them; but there was enough accommodation for it to be used as the Battery Headquarters and billet for the officers. Some of the horses were also kept there, as it had horse-watering facilities. A security picquet was also established there during the night to block the roads

**British Field Gunners awaiting orders. Their gun can be compared with the RHA 13-pounder on page 61.**

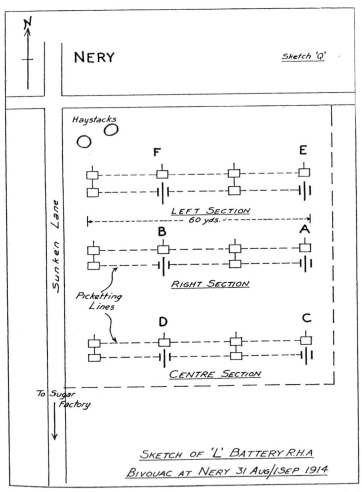

**Map 9. Sketch of L Battery gun lines on 31 August 1914. L Battery had time on the evening of 31 August 1914 to lay out its gun lines as per the Drill Book. This was the first time it was done during the Retreat.**

to the south and the southeast. The Battery Sergeant Major and his Number Ones (the sergeants in charge of each gun sub-section) as well as some of the specialists (signallers and farriers) made their quarters among the haystacks in the north of the field. The rest of the men stretched out in the gun lines.

On the early morning of 1 September the field, which runs south from the crossroads on the south side of Néry, was a scene of vigorous

**The crossroads at Néry today with the memorials to L Battery and the Queens Bays.**

activity. All the men of L Battery were busy preparing their 200 horses and their six 13 pounder guns and limbers for an early morning departure (as they had for each of the previous ten days, since the Retreat from Mons had begun). The field slopes away sharply to the south and east and was partly grassed and partly cultivated for sugar beet. The field had already been cleared of hay and this had been stacked as a number of haystacks at the top end of the field.

The Battery lines had been laid out very neatly for the night, with each section of two guns and their horses and limbers in line. This was the first time that this had been done on the Retreat and is an indication of how secure the battery felt themselves in the Néry position. Following Reveille at 2.30am, the Battery was prepared for moving out at 4.30am. Because of the dense mist prevailing that morning, Brigade

**L Battery Field looking south towards the sugar factory from the crossroads.**

Headquarters ordered a standstill until 5am, which was extended until 5.30am. The Battery had been ready to move at 4.30am, but on the 'stand fast' order, the poles were lowered (to take the weight off the horses shoulders) and sections of horses were led off to the sugar factory for watering, while some of the men then took advantage of the additional time to prepare breakfasts, wash themselves or groom horses. All battery personnel were mounted on their own horses, so the saddled ride-horses of the detachment numbers were tied to the gun or limber wheels by their head ropes.

The Battery Commander and his officers walked up from the sugar factory to the haystacks at about 5am. Major Sclater-Booth then left the officers there and went on with his bugler, Private Harry Goold, to Brigade Headquarters in the Mairie to receive further orders. When he arrived he met the Brigadier and his Brigade Major, together with the brigade French liaison officer, Lieutenant Raoul Johnston (who was later killed at Zillebecke, near Ypres, in May 1915). Lieutenant Colonel Pitman had just left to return to the 11th Hussars, having informed him of the reports (brought in by Lieutenant Tailby) of the German cavalry on the eastern heights. Almost immediately (at about 5.40am) shells began bursting over the village and rifle and machine gun fire was directed from the eastern plateau at the village. One of the shells actually came through the roof of the Mairie and Briggs was able to pick up the time fuze and verify that it was German and set for 800 metres. This provided all the confirmation he needed, and he immediately sent off two motor cyclists to Major General Allenby (commanding the Cavalry Division) at St. Vaast and Major General Snow (commanding 4th Infantry Division) at Verberie, advising them that he had been attacked by German cavalry, strength unknown.

Immediately the attack opened, Major Sclater-Booth left Brigade Headquarters with his young bugler and headed back to his battery. He attempted to return the way he had come down the main road, but a crowd of the Queen's Bays horses, frightened by the shelling, which had also landed in the Queen's

A gun crew poses beside their 13-pounder, the standard equipment of the RHA. The sergeant is kneeling at the trail in the No. 1 position and the Bombardier is sitting in the right-hand firing seat.

Bays quarters, were stampeding up this road, and he was forced to make his way back via a side road. Then a shell exploded among the stampeding horses, killing most of them and leaving their bloody bodies blocking the main road. Just as he was approaching the battery through a field of beet, a shell landed near him and knocked him unconscious. His trumpeter, Private Goold, was also blown to the ground, but scrambled to his feet, ran to the field and managed to blow the alarm, although the battery needed little alerting by this time. Major Sclater-Booth remained unconscious in the beet field until about 11am, when the Queen's Bays' rear party picked him up, just before the village was finally evacuated.

Captain Bradbury was standing with the other officers among the haystacks when the bombardment began. With him were two of the section officers, Lieutenant JD Campbell and Lieutenant LFH Mundy. The third section officer, Lieutenant J Giffard, was away trotting up a lame horse in the sunken road beside the bivouac. The surprise of the attack can hardly have been greater. Some guns had been seen moving earlier on the ridge, but they were thought to be French. The Germans had opened up with machine gun and rifle fire and with devastating artillery fire from their three batteries on the fields on the south side of the village where the Queen's Bays' horses and L Battery, which were the most exposed units, were caught in the open. The horses of F sub-section were away down at the sugar factory being watered, but the rest of the battery's horses were standing in march order with their poles down. The effect of shrapnel exploding among the horses and men was horrific, the shells burst among the harnessed horses causing them to panic and plunge, which drove their lowered poles into the ground, trapping them until they were all shot down. One team dragged its gun

Account of the practical (1) annihilation of "L" Batt<sup>y</sup> / Royal Horse Artillery, at NÉRY, OISE. on 1st Sept<sup>r</sup>. 1914.

At 4.30 a.m., we w.e.e, as ordered, ready to move, when we received fresh orders to "offsaddle, be ready to march at 15 minutes notice". After "offsaddling" we commenced watering our horses by subsection i.e the complement of horses for one Gun, two ammunition Wagons and ten Gunners. (in all 36 to 40 horses). My Subsection ("F") was in no. 4 position; watering commenced from the left flank of the Battery, nos: 6 & 5 subsections had returned from Water and no. 4 (my horses) had just gone to water (some 500 yards away) when I noticed some guns, dimly outlined in the fog on our right flank about 700 yards distant, moving quite slow slowly; thinking that they were French, I presumed inspecting me

**A page from Sergeant Nelson's diary.**

into the sunken road where it overturned and trapped them. The terrified and maddened horses could not be released easily from their harnesses and were killed. The only horses which were saved were from Lieutenant Giffard's D and C sub-sections, which had not been hooked in after watering, and those from the F sub-section, which were watering at the sugar factory.

The bombardment immediately transformed the scene from one of impeccable military order to devastation and chaos, as limbers and wagons were overturned or destroyed and men and horses were hit by bullets and shrapnel. Within seconds the Battery had almost ceased to exist as shells exploded overhead hitting the lines of unprotected men and horses. Sergeant Nelson has left a graphic account of the mayhem in the field.

*During the awful carnage the groaning of dying men and horses was audible amidst the terrific thundering of the cannon, the scenes were in most cases beyond description. One man in full view of me had his head cut clean off his body, another was literally blown to pieces, another was practically severed at the breast, loins, knees and ankles. One horse had its head and neck completely severed from its shoulders. So terrific was the hail of shrapnel that I was bespattered with blood from men and horses.*

Instinctively, those men who were able to sought shelter from the shellfire among the haystacks, in the sunken road beside the battery field, or down at the sugar factory, where most of F sub-section had been watering its horses. However, Captain Bradbury, the Second-in-Command of the Battery, did not seek shelter. Overcoming his surprise, he instantly decided to lead the shocked gunners to fight back against the German attackers. Calling out, 'Come on! Who's for the guns?' he ran out from the haystacks and made for the scene of carnage around the guns followed by the other officers and about a dozen men.

**The Sugar Factory weigh-bridge at the entrance to the factory, as it is today.**

They ran to the smashed and intermingled gun teams and started trying to release the injured and maddened horses from their harnesses and began attempting to get the guns into action. Some of the wheels of the guns had been so smashed in the initial bombardment that the guns could not be brought into action. However, the horse gunners managed to release four guns and attempted to get them firing that morning.

Bombardier Frank Perrett had been shaving behind the D gun when the attack commenced, and has left a vivid description of the initial surprise and chaos and also of the quick recovery by the gunners.

*When the first salvo fell, Gunner Marsh, my Number 2, and I, were just finishing shaving in rear of our detachment horses, which were tied to the gun wheel. A shell dropped right amongst them and the explosion flattened us. Marsh was struggling, but I told him to lie still as I could see he was badly hit: a piece of shell had gone right through his back and disembowelled him. All hell seemed to be let loose, with shells raining in amongst men and horses, and the screams of the latter could be plainly heard in the din. Then Lieut. Campbell came running across and shouted 'get that gun into action!' He and I managed to release the detachment horses from our gun and limber wheels – they were all dead or dying – and we managed to swing the gun round. Lieut Campbell took the layer's seat and layed by open sights on the German guns, which were now clearly visible, and seemed very close. I opened the limber, threw some rounds by the gun and jumped into Number 2's seat. I set the range at 800 and slammed in a round. Campbell reported 'Ready' and I ordered 'Fire!' We observed the round to be over the target, so I dropped the range to 500 and set the fuze at 'shrapnel zero', loaded, and we fired again. Realising that zero fuze was dangerous to our men and horses in front I set the next round at fuze 1¹/₂. We began to get results. By this time more men came doubling across and took over Numbers 2 and 4, with others getting ammunition. As soon as a full detachment could be made up, Lieut Campbell called me to help him get another gun into action.*

Because Sergeant Nelson's gun was not limbered up to its horses, he was able to reach it quickly when the action started.

*I resumed inspecting one of my Ammunition Wagons, when presently a terrific and deadly shrapnel fire swept 'L' Battery, literally mowing down men and horses.*

*I took cover by the wagons, momentarily dumbfounded, and awaiting orders, but after a second volley of shrapnel, seeing no officers near, called Gunner Darbyshire and with his assistance unlimbered my gun and directed it on the enemy's guns and opened fire.*

*Just then Captain Bradbury, Lieut Mundy, Corpl Payne and Driver Osborne arrived, and we kept up a destructive fire for some time, Gnr Darbyshire and Dvr Osborne heroically carrying ammunition from other wagons to augment the supply already in the Gun limber.*

*Lieuts Campbell and Giffard, with others whose names I do not know, brought No 5 Gun ('D') into action, but as they were directly behind my Gun, their shooting at the German Guns was limited. However a squadron of German Cavalry appeared on the left, on which this gun turned its fire and repulsed them, when an enemy's shell wounded the two brave officers and killed the men helping them. This left only my gun in action, against eight guns of the enemy.*

Unfortunately, there is no further information about this cavalry charge from the left or exactly which gun dealt with the German cavalry. Such an attack could have been very serious, as any cavalry who got through in this area (where there is a track down from the escarpment), before the defences were organised, could have cut the battery to pieces, and then entered the southern end of Néry.

Gunner Darbyshire provided his own account of his part in the opening action by the F gun.

*Owing to heavy losses in our battery I had become limber gunner, and it was part of my special duty to see to the ammunition in the limbers. But special duties at a time like that don't count for much; the chief thing is to keep the guns going, and now it was a case of everyone striving his best to save the battery... As soon as we got No. 6 gun into action I jumped into the seat and began firing, but so awful was the concussion of our own explosions and the bursting German shells that I could not bear it for long. I kept it up for about twenty minutes, then my nose and ears were bleeding because of the concussion, and I could not fire any more, so I left the seat and got a change by fetching ammunition.*

Lieutenant Giffard who, according to the account by Major Rodwell, had been in the sunken road beside the battery field trotting a lame horse when the action began, brought the third gun into action. He ran to the B sub-section gun with Sergeant Phillips and Gunner Richardson. They just managed to get the gun into action and fired perhaps eight rounds when they suffered a direct hit, which killed Gunner Richardson and wounded most of the detachment. Lieutenant Giffard and Sergeant Phillips carried on until another shell shattered one of the wheels and capsized the gun, killing Sergeant Phillips, and severely wounding Lieutenant Giffard. He was able to drag himself to the cover of the haystacks, but was wounded again on the way there. Lieutenant Giffard eventually recovered from his wounds and was awarded the Legion of Honour.

Finally, Bombardier Perrett related how he and Lieutenant Campbell, having handed over the D sub-section gun to a makeshift detachment, ran to get the fourth gun, the C sub-section gun, into action:

*We doubled to 'C' Sub's gun, loosened the traces from the dead and wounded horses, got the gun round and into action. Lieutenant Campbell jumped into the layer's seat, Gunner Miller did Number Two, another Gunner took Number Four, and I knelt at the trail as Number One, while Driver Mansfield and some others brought up ammunition.*

At the D sub-section gun, Sergeant Fortune and the others had barely begun firing when they were hit by a shell, which killed or wounded most of the detachment. Sergeant Fortune was mortally wounded and unable to move, but according to Lieutenant Colonel Gillman's account he was instrumental in getting some of the gunners and drivers under cover.

Bombardier Perrett continued his story of the events at the C gun:

*We quickly commenced firing, but it didn't last long. Suddenly there was a blinding flash and for a time I remembered no more, but soon came to in a dazed condition to find Mr. Campbell binding a field dressing round my head. A shell had burst right*

**Driver Drain, who was at Néry, places a wreath on the Néry gun in the Imperial War Museum, on behalf of L Battery, which was on service in India.**

*in front of our shield and a piece had got me in the face. Miller was killed and Mansfield was badly wounded.*

Amazingly, the C gun had actually been hit directly on the muzzle, rendering it totally unusable. It still stands today in the Imperial War Museum, London, where it is known as 'The Néry Gun'. It remains a silent witness to the terrific carnage at Néry, displaying the terrible damage to its wheels, shield and muzzle. Each year, on the anniversary of the battle, the Director of the Museum and a representative of the Royal Artillery place a poppy wreath on the Gun.

The battery field was suffering a storm of high explosive and shrapnel, which cut everything to pieces. Despite brave efforts by their crews, B, C and D guns had been knocked out, leaving just the F gun in action. Having done what he could for the wounded at the C gun, Lieutenant Campbell then moved on to help at the F gun, which was the only one still firing. Although wounded, he helped for a while with the ammunition and then took over the firing seat from Gunner Darbyshire.

At the F gun, Lieutenant Mundy was hit in the right shoulder but carried on observing the shots and using his left hand to feed ammunition. Then a German shell exploded near the shield, killing Lieutenant Campbell and fatally wounding Corporal Payne and Lieutenant Mundy. Lieutenant Mundy had been hit again badly in the right leg and collapsed near the trail. Captain Burnyeat of I Battery reported that after the battle he saw Lieutenant Mundy being carried away, 'his red face smiling and as cheerful as ever', but he did not recover from his grievous wounds and died in the hospital at Baron two days later.

Sergeant Nelson described how the exploding shell wounded him and the two officers as well as Corporal Payne:

*Lieut Campbell (though already wounded) came to our assistance, but ere long a German shell burst close to us, wounding him and also fatally wounding Lieut Mundy and Corpl Payne, also wounding me on the right side and slightly in the right leg and piercing my cap.*

Gunner Darbyshire also witnessed the end of Lieutenant Campbell:

*Immediately after I left the seat, Lieutenant Campbell, who had been helping with the ammunition, took it and kept the firing up without loss of a second of time. But he had not fired more than a couple of rounds when a shell burst under the shield. The explosion was awful, and the brave young officer was hurled about six yards away from the very seat in which I had been sitting a few seconds earlier. He lived for only a few minutes.*

Bombardier Perrett, whose head wound had been bound up by Lieutenant Campbell before he went off to help with the F gun, had passed out for a while and regained consciousness to find Lieutenant Campbell lying dead nearby:

*...another round burst in front of the gun and I was flung down with pieces of shrapnel in my back. I flaked out for what seemed an age, but I suppose it was only a few moments, and when I came round Lieutenant Campbell was lying dead across the trail. Machine guns were now spraying everything that moved, man and horse alike. Realising that where I lay I was in danger of more flying fragments, I tried to crawl under the gun, but the machine-gunners spotted me and I got one through the arm, which fractured the bone. I always think that was a lucky bullet, for if I had not dropped I should certainly have been riddled. One bullet struck an oil-bottle (brass) in my riding-pants pocket and glanced off.*

Clearly anyone who could not get under cover in that field risked further wounds or death. However, despite the injuries to most of the gun detachment, the F gun had still not been silenced by the German fire. The Battery Sergeant Major had run forward and now joined the remnants of the gun team. Sergeant Nelson was losing strength from a splinter in his chest and Captain Bradbury ordered him to retire to cover and get his wound dressed. He refused, saying that they had not many rounds left, so he 'might as well see the thing through'. Sergeant Nelson continued his account:

> There were now three serving the Gun, Capt Bradbury, Sergt Major Dorrell (who up to now had been using a rifle under cover) and myself, twice wounded; we still maintained a quick rate of deadly accurate fire until the ammunition supply began to wane and the two men carrying it to us disappeared.

The problem with the ammunition supply was that it was in wagons at least twenty yards away from the gun, and collecting it meant crossing an open space swept by machine gun fire and shrapnel. Both Darbyshire and Osborne were doing their best to keep the gun supplied, but could not keep up with the rate of fire. Captain Bradbury decided that they had to have more ammunition and went to get it himself. Sergeant Nelson related what happened next in his usual blunt fashion:

> Capt Bradbury went to get ammunition from an adjacent wagon, but he only got about four yards from the gun when a

**In this famous Matania painting, Sergeant Major Dorrell, Sergeant Nelson and Captain Bradbury are depicted serving the F Gun.**

*shell from the enemy completely cut both his legs off midway between knees and body, thus leaving SM Dorrell and myself in action.*

Gunner Darbyshire's account provides more sympathetic detail about how Captain Bradbury received his mortal injury.

*When I felt a little better I began to help Driver Osborne to fetch ammunition from the wagons. I had just managed to get back to the gun, with an armful of ammunition, when a lyddite shell exploded behind me, threw me to the ground, and partly stunned me.*

*When I came round I got up and found that I was uninjured. On looking round, however, I saw that Captain Bradbury, who had played a splendid part in getting the guns into action, had been knocked down by the same shell that floored me, and was mortally wounded. Though the Captain knew that death was very near, he thought of his men to the last, and begged to be carried away, so that they should not be upset by seeing him, or hearing*

*the cries which he could not restrain.*

Bombardier Perrett was also lying severely wounded nearby. His account confirms the fine example of unselfish behaviour and leadership in adversity continually shown by Captain Bradbury, despite his suffering from truly terrible injuries:

> *I was lying under the brakeshield of the gun inside the wheel, completely dazed, when suddenly there was another crash and something was blown right alongside the wheel. It was Captain Bradbury. He was grievously wounded: the shell had carried away both legs at the knee. As we lay beside each other he spoke quite rationally, asked about my wounds, called to Giffard and Mundy, and shouted encouragement to the other two, and now and then raised himself by grasping the spokes of the wheel to observe the shots. But at times he would grip the spokes and beat his stumps on the ground in agony. It was sheer guts that kept him rational.*

The gunners of L Battery kept up their effort until some time before 8am. It was then that I Battery arrived and began firing. Estimates of the damage done to the German guns by L Battery vary. Some of the onlookers thought they had destroyed three guns and later Captain Burnyeat, who inspected them, thought that only three of the German guns were worth bringing away. Certainly the shrapnel shells fired by L Battery must have caused significant casualties among the enemy gunners. Sergeant Nelson claimed that they silenced all the enemy guns:

> *We fired the two rounds remaining with the gun, and with them silenced the only German gun which appeared to be shooting, when 'I' Battery RHA opened fire from a position behind us and completed their destruction.*

Gunner Darbyshire also finished his account with a very emotive description of I Battery coming into action:

> *The three of us had served the gun and kept it in action till it was almost too hot to work, and we were nearly worn out. But we kept on firing, and with a good heart, for we knew that the Germans had been badly pounded, that the Bays had them in their grip, and that another battery of horse-gunners was dashing to the rescue. On they came in glorious style. There is no finer sight than a horse battery galloping into action. Two or three miles away from us, I Battery had heard the heavy firing and knew that something must have happened to us. Round they turned, and on they dashed, taking everything before them and*

*stopping for nothing till they reached a ridge about 2,000 yards away; then they unlimbered and got into action, and never was there sweeter music than that which greeted the three of us who were left in L Battery when the saving shells of I screamed over us and put the finish to the German rout.*

Actually, although the description of I Battery's guns sweeping into action and opening up as L Battery ceases firing is very colourful, it is improbable that this is exactly what happened. Gunner Darbyshire was unlikely to have been able to witness the coming into action of I Battery which, according to Captain Burnyeat, came into an open position, still in mist, twice before it opened fire about 1,200 yards from the German guns. While from both the Nelson and Darbyshire accounts it sounds as if L Battery kept firing almost right up to the time that I Battery opened fire, there actually appears to have been a significant gap in the time after L Battery ceased firing and before I Battery opened fire. Sergeant Nelson says that after he and BSM Dorrell stopped firing, he joined up with the firing line of the Queen's Bays:

*seeing the 'Bays' in action I took up a rifle and fired at some straggling German Infantry, I believe accounting for two of them. The 'kicking' of the rifle greatly intensified the pain in my right side and also increased the bleeding so I had to drop the rifle.*

Sergeant Nelson then went on to fill some ammunition belts for the Queen's Bays and help some of the wounded from the Battery, until he

**Camouflaged 13 pdr QF gun with its limber and gun crew.**

had his own wound dressed. Sergeant Major Dorrell, who was unwounded, was mounted on a horse and sent off by Brigadier-General Briggs with instructions to direct any batteries he found to open fire on the German guns. Both of the activities performed by Sergeant Nelson and Sergeant Major Dorrell after leaving the gun would seem to indicate that there was a significant gap between the firing of the last shell by L Battery and the opening of fire by I Battery.

Nevertheless the fire of L Battery undoubtedly caused damage to the German gun crews but as they were firing shrapnel, they probably would have done only limited damage to the guns themselves; although a number of the accounts indicate that at least three guns were put out of action. Only after October 1914 were the British artillery given fifty per cent HE shells, so that they could inflict much more damage on enemy equipment and positions. In any event the combined effect of the shellfire by L Battery and the thousands of rounds fired from the machine guns and rifles of the cavalry effectively prevented the German gunners from getting close to their guns. According to Lieutenant Colonel Wilberforce, commanding the Queen's Bays,

> by degrees... the eight guns...ceased firing and when the mist cleared and we could see the guns distinctly, every time anyone came near them the Vickers and all the rifles we had slated them with fire until the Germans gave up all attempts either to serve them or to get them away.

J. M. Brereton, in his account in Blackwood's Magazine, used Bombardier Perrett's words to describe the events near the end of the action, when men of D Company of the 1st Middlesex arrived.

> When the infantry relief arrived on the scene the German guns were silent, and so was the British 13-pdr. The last round gone, BSM Dorrell was slumped forward in the layer's seat to the left of the piece, head against the shield; Sergeant Nelson on the opposite seat was bent over the breech, his tunic front soaked with blood from his chest wound. Both men were numbed, and unbelieving that their ordeal was over. The men of the Middlesex were horrified at the carnage, and could only marvel that a single gun had still been in action among the shambles of dead and wounded men and horses, some of whom had been blown apart by the shellfire.

As the action ended, a corporal of the Middlesex found Captain Bradbury and Bombardier Perrett still lying by the gun wheel where they had both fallen.

> He offered his water-bottle to Bradbury who immediately

*passed it to the Bombardier; but the latter could not drink because of his scarred and swollen face, so Bradbury took a few gulps and then sank back. Meanwhile Sergeant Nelson, coughing up blood, had found some unwounded men who brought a door from the village and laid Bradbury on it. Before they carried him away, the Captain ordered them to cover up his lower body with a saddle blanket to hide his ghastly stumps, and made them promise to return for Perrett. On his way to the first-aid post (next to the village cemetery) the party happened to pass the Commanding Officer of the Bays, Lieutenant-Colonel Wilberforce, and Bradbury still had strength to call out, with a wry grin: 'Hello Colonel, they've hotted us up a bit, haven't they!' There was nothing that could be done for him, and knowing he was doomed, he asked to be taken inside the cemetery walls so that the other wounded should not witness his agony. And there among the tombstones of the departed peasantry, died a very gallant gentleman of the Royal Horse Artillery.*

**Captain Edward Bradbury VC.**

Despite this account of the end of Captain Bradbury, it seems that he was not left to die alone in the cemetery. After the battle all the battery wounded, including Bombardier Perrett, were taken off in ambulances to a temporary military hospital at Baron. The dead had been identified and gathered together, but had to be left unburied as the Germans were coming. Apparently this did not include Captain Bradbury who was found still alive (but dying) in the cemetery by Colour-Sergeant E M Lyons of the Warwickshire Regiment:

*As we got near the village most distressing sights met us. On the roadside there were turned-over limbers complete with teams of poor horses all killed trying to escape and just off the roadside were lying the bodies of the drivers. I felt very sad. In the village I assisted the RAMC men to load up the ambulances. After the last ones went off I was still scouting around to make sure there were no more wounded. There was one we couldn't put in the ambulance he was so badly wounded so we borrowed a farm cart and packed it with straw and made him as comfortable as possible. It was the battery commander, Capt. Bradbury, who I'm sorry to say died soon.*

Captain Edward Bradbury still lies in that cemetery in Néry, together with Lieutenant John Campbell and some of the men from the Battery who were killed with them. He was a popular officer who led by example. His determination, leadership and fearless action was a major reason why the Battery pulled itself together and continued to fight back against the overwhelming numbers of the German artillery and machine guns. In so doing, not only did they spoil the key offensive effort of the Germans, but drew a major part of the German fire onto themselves.

The six guns of L Battery, of which only four got the chance to fire back, were not only outnumbered by the twelve heavier German guns, but could only fire shrapnel shells. This made them less effective than the German guns, which fired both shrapnel and high explosive shells. Nevertheless, their fire was effective enough to force the Germans to concentrate all their guns to the south of Néry to overcome their resistance. According to the author of the account of the German *18th Dragoons* the ability of the guns of L Battery to fire back effectively was a surprise:

> *Our rapid approach to Néry had not been noticed by the enemy, so our attack took him completely by surprise. The British were having a comfortable morning wash and brush-up when our first shrapnel burst among them and our machine guns opened fire, causing a considerable amount of damage. The enemy, however, soon began a heavy artillery fire, and advanced in skirmishing order to meet us.*

No doubt the Germans would have been able to do more if their ammunition had not been in limited supply, but even so, at the end of the battle, at least three of their guns were found to be still loaded. This confirms how difficult it was for the German gun crews to stay near the guns in the face of such determined counterfire from the British rifles and machine guns.

The resistance by the gunners of L Battery, against all the odds, was key to the survival of 1 Cavalry Brigade that morning. General von Garnier planned to subdue the resistance in Néry with shellfire on the centre of the target, and then capture it with the two enveloping wings of his cavalry attack. The continued resistance of L Battery spoilt this plan. In the end the effective return fire from the surviving gun forced the Germans to move all their artillery to the southeast firing point to attempt to overcome it. Even in that position they were not immune from the fire of the F gun and the machine guns of the Queen's Bays and 11th Hussars. As for the two German flank assaults, they were dealt with by both the defensive strength of the British cavalry and their mounted and dismounted counter attacks.

# Chapter Six

## THE COUNTER ATTACK BY THE 5TH DRAGOON GUARDS

The attack on 1 Cavalry Brigade commenced with the occupation of the crest of the high ground to the east of Néry by *3 Cavalry Brigade* (the *2nd Cuirassiers* and *9th Uhlans*) under command of Colonel Count von der Goltz. From that position, in the area behind the escarpment directly east of Néry, they would have been able to launch a direct attack on the east, or a flanking attack on the north, of the village. According to the account by General von Poseck, a detachment of the *Guard Machine Gun Company*, under the command of Captain von Schierstadt, was placed south of the brigade further along the crest, and a battery of four guns of the *3rd Artillery Battalion* was also placed in position on the crest east of Néry. Initially 3 Brigade tried a mounted assault. However, the steepness of the escarpment meant it was unable to progress beyond the edge of the escarpment and the brigade was forced to dismount and form a firing line east of the village, with its horses held well back behind the firing line.

The 5th Dragoon Guards were billeted in the houses in the northern area of the village. Their horses were grazing in the open in the field opposite the village cemetery, until they were saddled up ready for the move out. Like the other units, the 5th Dragoon Guards had been prepared to move out at 4.30am, and their early morning patrol to the north of Néry had found no sign of any enemy. They had started to take advantage of the stand-down by off-saddling and preparing proper

**British Cavalryman carrying his highly effective Lee Enfield rifle.**

breakfasts, when Second Lieutenant Tailby and his patrol returned at about 5.30am. It is possible that due to their preparations for moving out they had withdrawn their roadblocks to the north and north east of Néry, as Second Lieutenant Tailby did not report any hold-up when he returned to Néry via the Bethisy St. Pierre road. However, he did feel it necessary to send Corporal Parker to warn the 5th Dragoon Guards of the presence of enemy cavalry close by. Apparently, the 5th Dragoon Guards started to 'stand to', but then it was decided that this warning was probably yet another 'spook' report by the 11th Hussars, and they laughingly returned to their previous occupations.

When the attack by the Germans began, the 5th Dragoon Guards were largely protected from injury by the angle of the village, but quite a number of the horses stampeded (and were collected later by the 3rd Hussars). The Commanding Officer, Lieutenant Colonel George Kirkpatrick Ansell, having ordered them to secure what horses they could and man their 'stand to' stations, went to Brigade Headquarters for orders.

Despite the surprise attack, Brigadier-General Briggs was an experienced commander, and able to gather his forces swiftly and make a plan to conduct a robust defence. Initially, he is said to have thought the attack was by a comparatively weak enemy force. He needed to ensure that he had a reserve and, as the 11th Hussars were clearly in a good defensive position, and well able to hold the eastern side of the village, he ordered Lieutenant Colonel Pitman to secure the eastern side of the village with his B and C Squadrons, and send his A Squadron to him to act as the Brigade Reserve. Then, to regain the initiative, he ordered Lieutenant Colonel Ansell to secure the north side of the village and to use his mounted squadrons to make a turning movement on the left of the German force. Despite losing a large number of horses in the initial stampede, Ansell was able to mount most of his A and B Squadrons and led them off, leaving C Squadron and his Machine Gun Section to occupy the houses and defend the northern end of the village.

The two squadrons were somewhat under strength, because of the loss of the stampeded horses, as Ansell led them around to the plateau north east of Néry, towards St. Luce Farm. One account says that A Squadron was left as a holding force north of the village, while Ansell approached the German forces with just B Squadron, while other accounts say that he crossed the gully and worked up the end of the spur and approached the German firing line with both squadrons. A Squadron manoeuvred near St. Luce Farm and B Squadron, further to its left, came upon the led horses of *3 Brigade*. Apparently, during this approach to the enemy they came under heavy artillery and machine gun fire. When they reached the top of the ridge they dismounted and employed their rifles to deadly effect, particularly against the Germans' led horses. Ansell, who was directing operations from his horse, was mortally wounded during this part of the action; his dying order to the men, who carried him back to cover, was to return at once to the firing line.

The Second–in-Command of the Regiment, Major Winwood, then took over command. Eventually the 5th Dragoon Guards received the order to withdraw back to Néry from Briggs, as he apparently thought that the situation in the village had become critical. However, by the time the two squadrons actually returned, the action was over and the Germans had withdrawn. This flank action by the 5th Dragoon Guards seems to have lasted for almost two hours.

Although the attack by the 5th Dragoon Guards is not well documented, it was certainly effective in preventing *3 Brigade* succeeding with its attack. The British attacking force was small, but the mist probably hid its inferiority in numbers from the Germans. The *9th Uhlans'* report says that because of the mist the regiments and squadrons of *3 Brigade* became intermingled and command was very difficult. Eventually, the whole of *3 Brigade* seems to have been in the firing line along the crest of the hill, supported by the machine guns and some of the guns of the mounted artillery, where it came under fire from both the 5th Dragoon Guards and the 11th Hussars. The account in the regimental history of the *9th Uhlans* stresses the shock felt by the dismounted Germans in the firing line that the British should shoot into the led horses! As a result of this fire, the horse holders were unable to retain control of them and a large number ran off. Sergeant Hensling only just managed to save the regimental standard of the *9th Uhlans*. It also records the fact that five members of the Regiment, including Oberleutnant von Zitzewitz, Gefreiter Dahms and three uhlans were killed on 1 September. Actual losses by *3 Brigade* are uncertain but a realistic estimate is that total casualties were of the order of around a hundred, of which at least seven were killed, and sixty-two were captured (of which possibly over half were wounded); and perhaps at least another thirty wounded were taken away in carts. Clearly, morale was also affected by the loss of the led horses, which was a very significant blow to the dismounted cavalrymen. Many of them were obliged to leave sitting in carts or were forced to surrender, as they could not get away. Confirmation of the severity of the losses

suffered is conveyed in the *9th Uhlans* account of their situation after
the battle:

> *The concentration of the Regiment after the battle made a
> very sad picture. It was only possible to round up a few of the
> led horses, which had stampeded. Anyone who could get hold
> of a horse, regardless of which Squadron or Regiment to which
> it belonged, just sat on it. The majority of our troopers were
> unmounted, but were made somewhat mobile by putting them
> into requisitioned farm wagons. The dead, unfortunately had to
> be left behind unburied, the wounded were taken with us on the
> wagons.*

There were a number of gallant actions by the 5th Dragoon Guards
during this attack on the German right flank, which successfully
limited the mounted attack by the Germans developing on the north
side of Néry. Exceptional boldness shown by Corporal Peach and
Sergeant Langford resulted in both being awarded the DCM for their
actions. Sergeant Langford, on the left flank of the attack, charged up
to within a hundred yards of the German firing line, and then,
dismounting his troop, killed one officer, nine uhlans and sixteen
horses with rifle fire (these figures are partially confirmed by the
German casualty lists). Sergeant Langford then led his troop round to
the flank, where they continued to engage the German firing line.
Corporal Peach showed the greatest daring and coolness in covering
the retirement of the regiment, and relieved the pressure on his troop
by a turning movement with his section, which resulted in all the men
being put out of action, except himself, although it ensured the survival
of the rest of the troop.

Lieutenant Colonel Ansell, whose bold leadership was critical,
lies buried in Verberie Military Cemetery together with six of his
Dragoons. In addition, another officer attached to the 5th Dragoon
Guards, Lieutenant Maurice Hill, also took part in the attack around
St. Luce and was reported killed. His body, with his face covered in
blood, was brought in and laid beside Colonel Ansell on the ground.
According to Pitman's 1920 account, a most curious incident then
followed.

> *The tide of battle flowed over them. In the afternoon of
> September 1, a woman who was a staymaker in Paris and who
> happened to be on holiday to her mother and father in a
> neighbouring village, thought she might go up to Néry and see
> for herself where the fight had been. She found Hill still
> unburied, and saw that he was alive. She managed to get a cart,*

L Battery and Queen's Bays plot in the Verberie Military Cemetery. In the top left can be seen the headstones of the graves of Lieutenant Colonel Ansell and six of the men from 5th Dragoon Guards killed in the St Luce attack.

*took him to her house, and when the French some days later drove the Germans back, she reported the fact to a French officer. Hill had remained unconscious most of the time. The French evacuated him when the Aisne fighting was drawing to a close, and the new CO of the 5th Dragoon Guards received an intimation from the French at Paris to say that Hill was in hospital there. (He had of course been reported dead and his identity disc taken from him).*

*One of his brother officers was sent to Paris to identify him. The French found out who he was by means of a pair of boots he had on, made by Peal. They wrote to Messrs Peal and quoted the number.*

*Lieut. Hill's recovery was very slow. His memory had completely gone, and he had to start re-learning his alphabet. He is now almost entirely recovered.*

The 5th Dragoon Guards lost their Commanding Officer and six men killed, together with another two officers and eleven men wounded, in the action at Néry. Certainly, their action in taking the battle to *3 Brigade* broke up that potentially dangerous attack and prevented 1 Cavalry Brigade from being overwhelmed from the north. It is remarkable that this bold action was undertaken by two scratch squadrons riding into the mist and fearlessly engaging superior numbers of the enemy where they found them.

# Chapter Seven

# THE QUEEN'S BAYS COUNTERATTACK AT THE SUGAR FACTORY

Like L Battery, the 2nd Dragoon Guards (The Queen's Bays), were billeted on the south side of Néry. The men of A and B Squadrons were accommodated in buildings, but their horses and the men of C

**Map 10. 1 Cavalry Brigade solidifies its defence against German attacks East and South of Néry. 2 Squadrons 5 DGs attack German 3 Cavalry Bde from North West and halt that attack. 11th Hussars establish strong defence in east of village and with MGs dominate the ridge opposite. Queen's Bays establish a firing line with their MGs and rifles along the sunken road. L Bty gets some of its guns into action and shells the German guns.**

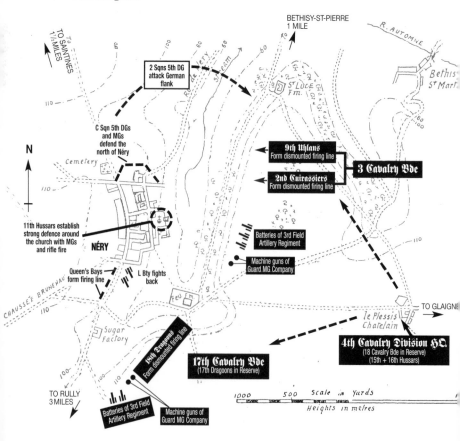

Squadron were bivouacked in the open field south of Néry. This was across the Rully road from where L Battery was billeted in the cornfield, with its guns, neatly but vulnerably lined up in sections.

The initial salvos of enemy gunfire hit the horses of the Queen's Bays and L Battery with devastating effect. Lieutenant Archie Lamb recorded the shocking start to the morning in his diary:

*Shortly after 6 am, I was just going to shave, when a heavy fire was suddenly opened on us by German guns close up to us (within 800 yards of the village). We were thoroughly surprised, and the first few shells got right in amongst the horses of 'C' Squadron, which were fastened up in lines with them. All my men ran towards the further end of the village under cover of a high wall. The horses of 'B' Squadron, and I believe 'A' Squadron began to stampede.*

Those Queen's Bay's horses which were not killed or badly injured, tried to flee the noise and danger and stampeded up the main road of Néry. Unfortunately they ran straight into more shellfire and a large number were killed in the main road almost outside the Mairie.

According to Trooper Clarke of the Queen's Bays, it was impossible to stop the horses running away;

*I remember the morning as being very misty. We had orders to saddle up but because of the mist we couldn't move so we stood down and we had breakfast and watered the horses. Suddenly we heard the sound of an explosion and then a barrage of shells. I think it was something like 5 in the morning. We rushed to see what was happening and*

**Trooper William Clarke of B Squadron, Queen's Bays. This photograph of the 18 year old was taken just before the outbreak of war. His good luck at the sugar factory continued during four years of service in and out of the trenches.**

Soldiers of the Queen's Bays in barracks in 1919 together with some children. Trooper Clarke on the far right looks much older than his years.

*found the shells had burst amongst our horses. I think they were C Squad's. A lot of them were terribly injured and killed and a lot of them stampeded off with fright. There were men holding on to them but they couldn't halt them. We had no idea what was really happening. Some of our blokes improvised a firing line and the gunners dragged some of their guns into action. By this time other horses of my Squad 'B' and 'A's were stampeding after 'C' Squad's horses.*

Despite the panic of the horses and the severe casualties to the men who were caught in the open (at least twenty men were killed or wounded), the Queen's Bays recovered very

The former sugar factory from the south approach today.

The sugar factory as it looked at the time of the battle.

**The field behind the Sugar factory where the German guns were placed, as seen from Feu Farm on the right.**

quickly. Lieutenant Colonel Herbert Wilberforce quickly organised the defence of the south of the village, with Majors Harmon and Ing establishing a robust defence with their squadrons along the Rully road. Lieutenant Archie Lamb and the available men of his machine gun troop ran down to position themselves along the bank of the sunken road, just near the cross roads close to the haystacks in the corner of the L Battery field. From the cover of this sunken road, the machine gunners and the troopers who joined them with their rifles, were able to aim very effective fire at the German batteries and dismounted cavalry, and suffered very few casualties themselves. Lamb described how quickly they reacted to the surprise attack and formed the firing line, which was to be so effective in resisting the German attacks:

> As soon as we realised the direction of the enemy's fire, I collected some of my machine gunners, and brought my guns into action at the south end of the village on the Rully road. We were under heavy artillery fire and rifle fire now to the end of the battle. Luckily, none of the men who were with me were hit whilst we were getting the guns into position. I was very shorthanded as I could not collect all my gunners. They had scattered during the first alarm and were in different parts of the village. However, the six men I had with me showed great bravery and the guns were soon fixed up on the side of the road which runs through a small cutting about two feet deep, affording a certain amount of cover from the enemy's fire. Various men and officers lined this bank, and formed quite a good firing line. The enemy, under cover of the early morning mist, had brought their guns up on to a plateau commanding the village, and only about 700 yards away from it.

Despite the early morning mist, the flash of the German guns could be seen, from the Rully road, perhaps just 400-500 yards away across the

British infantry forming a firing line along a ditch in 1914.

small valley on the other side of the escarpment. Lance Corporal Frederick Webb of the Queen's Bays, who was the Number One (the firer) on one of the machine guns, was the first into action. Despite the havoc caused by the enemy shells falling among the Queen's Bays, he had the presence of mind to grab one of the heavy machine guns from its carriage and unhesitatingly ran to a fire position near the corner of

Lieutenant Lamb and the two sections of his mounted machine gun troop in barracks. Lance Sergeant Webb is mounted on the extreme right of the photograph.

the sunken lane. The Queen's Bays were equipped with two machine guns, which were transported on gun carriages pulled by four horses. When dismounted, the guns were normally fired from a tripod mount. Lance Corporal Webb had seen the flash of the enemy guns, and did not wait for Fire Orders or for a tripod. He planted the Vickers machine gun on his knees and straightaway began hosing fire back at the German gun position, over the heads of the devastated L Battery. The Vickers is a heavy weapon (it weighs almost 30lbs without its tripod) and he appears to have used his knees as a rest to steady the machine gun. In any event this remarkable action quickly became part of the legend of the battle. Webb's rapid fire provided cover for the rest of the Queen's Bays to set

**Lance Sergeant Frederick Webb, pictured later in the war.**

The Corporals' Mess of the Queen's Bays pictured just before the war. Lieutenant Colonel Willoughby is in the centre of the front row and Lance Corporal Webb is standing at the far right of the back row.

The Certificate of the Mention in Despatches signed by Winston Churchill as Secretary of State for War in 1919.

up the other machine gun and to establish a rifle firing line along the lane. It also seems to have given the horse gunners some respite and enabled them to get to their own guns and begin releasing them and swinging them round to face the enemy fire.

Gunner Darbyshire, in the L Battery field, had also recovered quickly from the shock of the first rain of enemy shells, and helped Sergeant Nelson bring the F gun into action. He recorded the debt of gratitude that the horse gunners felt to the machine gunners of the Queen's Bays, and particularly to the extraordinary action of Lance Corporal Webb.

*The Bay's horses, like our own, had been either killed or wounded, or had bolted, but the men had managed to get down on the right of us and take cover under the steep bank of the road; from that position, which was really a natural trench, they fired destructively. British cavalry, dismounted, did some glorious work in the Great War, but they did nothing finer, I think, than their work near Compiègne on that September morning. And of all the splendid work there was none more splendid than the performance of a lance-corporal who actually planted a machine gun on his knees and rattled into the Germans with it. There was plenty of kick in the job, but he held on gamely, and he must have done heavy execution with his six hundred bullets a minute.*

The courageous horse gunners were being decimated by the shells exploding around them as they attempted to release their guns and turn them on the enemy. Only the rapid firing of the two machine guns behind them provided any cover in that bare field. Eventually more of the Queen's Bays machine gun troop gathered around, brought up ammunition and set up the tripods. Then the Queen's Bay machine gunners could began the serious business of dominating the German positions, as they poured thousands of rounds into the German guns and dismounted cavalry over the chaotic shambles in L Battery's field. The continuous firing by the machine guns of the Queen's Bays was an undoubted battle winner for the British that morning, for as long as they were firing there was no way that the German cavalry could break through the southern flank of the Néry defences. Lance Corporal Webb was promoted to Lance Sergeant and Mentioned in Dispatches for his leadership and heroic example that morning.

Lieutenant Lamb, who spent most of his time filling gun belts and directing the fire of his two gun teams, was awarded the DSO for his leadership of the machine gunners and his men were awarded Mentions in Despatches. As he narrated later:

*We opened fire on the German guns, and my No. 1s showed great gallantry under a withering fire. The Horse Artillery Battery (L Battery) was standing formed up just to our right front, and got the full brunt of the enemy's artillery fire, which killed off practically all their horses and a big percentage of their men in just the first few minutes. However, those who were left soon got some of the guns into action, and did excellent work silencing the enemy's guns.*

*We continued to fire off thousands of rounds both at the guns and at their infantry, who were advancing through standing corn, and also at another body who were trying to work round our right flank. The battle lasted about two hours, by which time the enemy seemed to have had enough. They made repeated attempts to get their guns away but, owing to heavy fire, were unable to do so, and eventually they abandoned them.*

*Both my guns worked splendidly without a single jam, and the men who were with me working them have been noted by the Colonel for their good work, and will probably be mentioned in despatches.*

Due to the devastating effect of the opening German fire, which killed and wounded many men and dispersed others, just seven men were available to man the Queen's Bays' machine guns. They were:

| | |
|---|---|
| Lance Corporal Webb | No. 1 |
| Private Goodchild | No. 1 |
| Private Phillips | No. 2 |
| Private Fogg | No. 2 |
| Private Emmett | No. 3 |
| Private Ellicock | No. 3 |

In addition the two teams were aided by Private Horne, who was normally a driver but did excellent work fetching ammunition and water for the guns under heavy fire.

Despite their relatively vulnerable position on the edge of the L Battery field, the machine gunners were able to dominate the German positions with their concentrated fire and prevent any of the enemy attacks, of up to three regiments of dismounted cavalry, from developing successfully. They were under stiff fire from the enemy shells, machine guns and carbines, and were very fortunate not to become casualties themselves. Only Private Ellicock was unlucky enough to be hit as he moved around assisting with the ammunition supply, as Lieutenant Lamb explained in his account:

*Ellicock was hit in the shoulder whilst assisting with the ammunition boxes, and about five minutes later was shot through the neck and was taken away on a broken down door.*

Ellicock died later that month in a military hospital in England, but was awarded the Distinguished Conduct Medal for his action that day.

Major Harman, commanding A Squadron, organised the defence along the Rully road, together with Major Ing, commanding B Squadron of the Queen's Bays, thus securing the right of the brigade position. Major Ing sent Sergeant Fraser and two men down to the sugar factory to occupy it and picquet the approaches from the two

**Dead German infantry left behind in the German withdrawal**

roads which met there. They were eventually shelled out of the factory. The southern end of the village was barricaded and became the centre of 1 Cavalry Brigade's defence. Later, when the Germans apparently moved all their artillery right round to the south east flank, the 11th Hussars also moved their two machine guns round to the southern corner of their position, where they could support the fire of the Queen's Bays.

Lieutenant de Labouchere, the French liaison officer with the Queen's Bays, also ran down to join Lieutenant Lamb and his machine gun troop. In his 1933 account of the battle, he claimed that he told Lieutenant Lamb where the German guns were firing from:

*The flashes of discharge from the German guns were now easily seen between Feu Farm and Mont Cormont, and served as a target at a range of 800 metres (later corrected to about 500 metres).*

While Lieutenant de Labouchere was assisting the Queen's Bays machine guns, they were visited by Brigadier-General Briggs. Briggs was an active commander and conducted an inspection of all the defensive positions in the village, visiting all the units in turn, accompanied by Major Stephen Cawley, his Brigade Major. He was obviously concerned about the security of the southern flank, which seemed to be the focus of the German attacks. Lieutenant de Labouchere was very conspicuously dressed in his French Dragoon uniform, consisting of a plumed helmet, black tunic with white collar and cuffs, and red breeches. While visiting the Queen's Bays' machine gun position Briggs saw Lieutenant de Labouchere helping, and joked

89

**British infantry manning a Vickers machine gun mounted on its tripod. The No.1 is firing. The No.2 is feeding the cotton belts of 250 rounds into the gun. Further belts are carried in metal boxes. The bolt action .303 SMLE rifle, with which all British troops were equipped, is clearly shown slung over the shoulder of the soldier on the right.**

with him about the visibility of his uniform, which marked him out from the khaki figures around him and was attracting enemy fire.

*Then, as he had surprised him in the act of firing some belts of machine-gun ammunition, he asked him laughingly if he thought he was killing many Germans. The answer was, needless to say, strictly in the affirmative! Continuing his inspection, General Briggs went to see the gunners at L Battery, 100 metres away.*

It would appear that it was during this inspection of the L Battery position by the Brigadier and his Brigade Major that Major Cawley was mortally wounded by a shell fragment and carried to the side of the field. Lieutenant de Labouchere described the horrendous carnage among the men and horses in the Battery position, which was visible from their position at the side of the hay field.

*From the Queen's Bays' machine gun positions, the spectacle presented by the battery was horrifying. But those with the machine guns were so busy that that they hadn't time to look for long at the pathetic sight of its ripped-up horses, the wounded crawling along to get under cover of the straw stacks which had caught fire, and the wrecked guns and limbers. Among many other wounded, Major Cawley was to be seen being taken away on a stretcher, completely scalped by a shell and covered in blood. He was only destined to survive his fearful wound for a few minutes.*

Brigadier-General Briggs did not confine his actions to inspection of the firing positions. According to Captain Jack of the Cameronians, who was sent to offer help from his unit and arrived towards the end of the battle, he even took an active role with the machine gun :

*Near the eastern houses General Briggs, to whom I report, is assisting to man a Vickers gun. On a crest some 800 yards away twelve German field guns, now mute, face us.*

Lieutenant Colonel Wilberforce positioned himself in the centre of the Queen's Bays, defence position near the L Battery field and was able to observe the fire on the German positions and direct the defence of this flank. Although the Rully road provided plenty of cover against fire from the east, the southern flank was clearly a very dangerous place for the officers who needed to move around to control and inspire the defence, and many of them were wounded.

The German attack on the south of Néry was commenced by *17 Cavalry Brigade (17th* and *18th Mecklenburg Dragoons*). The *18th Dragoons* were originally ordered to make a mounted charge, but claimed that the nature of the ground made this impracticable, and so they had to dismount, leaving their horses in the rear of their position, while they formed a firing line and attacked on foot. Attacking on foot using the ground could have been a very sensible tactic for well-trained Jägers, but was not very successful for the dragoons. Unlike the British cavalry, who always practised firing rifles from a dismounted position, the German cavalry preferred to attack using their lances, swords or pistols from the saddle, and do not seem to have been very effective when reduced to using just their carbines.

In any case, the dragoons were not in good physical shape. Like all the other members of the division, they had been on the march since 2am the previous day and had had just one break of about two hours to feed the horses at Offémont the previous evening. The brigade was also under strength due to the hard combat it had seen in Belgium and each dragoon regiment would only have been able to field just over some 400 men. Of more concern to the Germans was their limited ammunition supply, due to the decision to leave behind much of the support transport. This meant that once they knew they could not be successful with a mounted charge, they were unlikely to be able to maintain a sustained fire fight and would eventually have had to husband their rate of fire.

Although *17 Cavalry Brigade* was assigned the southerly attack, the attack was initially undertaken by just the *18th Dragoons*, supported by the guns of the 3rd Artillery Battalion and the detachment of machine guns. Probably not all the guns were in position on the crest south east of Néry (just south of Feu Farm) from the start of the action. L Battery in its accounts reports that two guns were seen initially on the crest south east of Néry and two batteries were on the crest east of Néry. Possibly, just two guns were placed originally on this southerly position, and were gradually joined later by all the other guns. Certainly, the 11th Hussars account reported that the gun battery opposite them moved position to join up with the other guns.

Pitman, in his account of the battle, says that three batteries were in line just 400 yards (which was measured later) from the L Battery position. In his sketch of the battle, these twelve guns are shown on the heights east of the sugar factory. This location is confirmed by, for example, Lieutenant de Labouchere, who wrote that he saw the three batteries of twelve guns in action on the ridge south east of Néry. Norrie, who led the 11th Hussars troop, which charged the cleared German gun position, said in his 1967 lecture:

> One Battery of four guns may possibly have been in position North of Feu Farm, (Colonel Becke places them there – I am not prepared to dispute this), but certainly the other two, and personally I think, all three, were south east of Néry and Feu Farm.

The movement of the guns around the battlefield, as well as the effect of mist and smoke, may have been responsible for much of this confusion. Lord Norrie also reported what he saw at the end of the action when on the German gun position:

> There were eight guns in position flanked by two machine guns. As far as I remember, five guns were pointing in the direction of L and three in the direction of I.

A similar observation was made by Captain Burnyeat, who was responsible for shelling the German guns, and later found that three of the eight guns in the position had been turned in his direction to try to respond to his fire.

Initially, the *17th Dragoons* were not involved in the southern attack, but were kept in reserve at Le Plessis-Chatelain and possibly to

**German gun limbers and dead horses pictured after an encounter with the British.**

protect the open southern flank. Eventually their regimental record states that they were brought forward to support the artillery, which, 'in the early morning mist, had approached the enemy too closely'. Apparently this injudicious placing of the artillery made the gunners vulnerable to British fire and the *17th Dragoons* were ordered to come up to form a firing line to provide covering fire, while the gunners attempted to get some of the guns away. The battery of four guns, which was finally extracted, stayed with the *17th Dragoons,* until it was finally abandoned in the Forest of Ermenonville the following night. Apart from this action in support of their artillery, the *17th Dragoons* do not seem to have been very actively involved in the battle of Néry.

Realising that both of his attacking Brigades had got bogged down in their flanking attacks, General von Garnier attempted to settle the action by ordering a final attack on the left flank to take the south side of the village using the fresh *18 Brigade*. It is possible that he may also have ordered the massing of artillery and machine guns on the same fire position south east of Néry, so that twelve 77mm artillery pieces and six Maxim machine guns were available to support this final reinforced assault.

*18 (Hussar) Brigade*, was at pretty well full strength, as it was not involved in any of the serious actions in Belgium. So far that morning it had been kept in reserve, with the Divisional HQ at Le Plessis-Chatelain, behind the centre of the German attack. Colonel von Printz, commanding *18 Brigade,* decided that he would lead the charge from Le Plessis-Chatelain, with Lieutenant Colonel Ludendorf leading the *16th Hussars* and Lieutenant Colonel von Zieten commanding the *15th*

*Hussars*. He gave the command; 'Form up and charge. Follow me!' Due to the thick mist (and lack of reconnaissance reports) no one had a clear idea of the geography of the area or where or what they were charging. Lieutenant Colonel Ludendorf sensibly, if perhaps audaciously, asked if any reconnaissance would be made. Apparently the Brigade Orderly Officer, OberLeutnant Wilink, replied, saying; 'Certainly, during the advance!' This rather obviously turned out to be too late. Each regiment advanced in waves, the *16th Hussars* on the far left, with its 4th Squadron leading, *15th Hussars* advanced on the right (nearest the Gun line south east of Néry) with its 3rd and 4th Squadrons in the first wave, 2nd Squadron in the second wave and the 1st Squadron in troops echeloned in rear.

General von Poseck's account of the action which followed, is quite colourful:

> *The regiment (the 15th Hussars) attacked the English infantry in beet fields, disregarding the heavy infantry, artillery and machine gun fire, which it received in part from the right flank. In spite of heavy losses of both men and horses, the British infantry was overridden at a fast and spirited gallop, thanks to our East Prussian horses, which stood in fine fashion the strain of the attack. The purpose of the attack was attained. The infantry which had been overridden by the regiment was eliminated and the reserves which had been hurriedly brought out of the village had been stopped and brought to a halt. Now the regiment was ordered to dismount and attack the enemy with the carbine...*
>
> *Threatened on all sides, the English forces, much our superiors in numbers, had to be drawn back on the defences of their bivouac, and before the reserves, which were being brought up, could participate, the 4th Cavalry Division withdrew.*

In fact there were no British infantry in such a position as was described by von Poseck; and from the first hand accounts of the German officers who participated in this action, the attack seems to have been considerably less successful than described, principally due to the lack of reconnaissance, and confusion caused by the mist.

For the *16th Hussars*, who were supposed to be on the left of the charge, there was no success at all. According to their own regimental account after galloping for about five hundred metres, the attackers came across the sunken cart track, which disorganised the formation of the attack. Then a thousand metres later they came to the steep ravine, which they could not cross. (This ground description fits very well if riding due west from Le Plessis-Chatelain, and would have brought

Pte Liversidge (seated) was in B Squadron, Queen's Bays, and wounded early on the morning of 1 September while firing back at the Germans. He was evacuated to the hospital at Baron, captured by the Germans, but eventually released and made his way back to England. The picture was taken in 1917, but he never really recovered from his wounds (Doctors could not remove the bullet, which was too close to his spine) and he died in 1932.

them to the edge of the ravine almost directly east of Néry. However, it was rather a long way to maintain a gallop with tired horses, even East Prussian horses). Their advance to the ravine in the thick mist may be the origin of the report of a mounted squadron seen on the heights east of Néry by the 11th Hussars. If this supposition is true, it means that they had become truly lost in the mist, as they had began the attack on the left of the Hussar Brigade formation and had somehow swung far to the right. Anyway, a few riders on specially trained horses (apparently some horses had been trained to jump even though they could not see the ground on the far side of an obstacle) attempted to leap into the ravine. This intrepid action, resulting from a complete lack of reconnaissance and knowledge of the ground, was certainly brave, but foolhardy. It killed the horses that made the jump and injured their riders, including OberLeutnant Vasel and three hussars. In the event, these men survived their falls, managed to hide from the British after the battle, and eventually rejoined their regiment some days later.

The remainder of the leading squadron then dismounted and attempted to fire on the British positions with their carbines. By this stage, the *16th Hussars* must have moved well south of Néry, because they received very little return fire (probably only 'overs') and claimed that they saw an enemy battery coming into action only one hundred metres away (this can only have been I Battery). The report seems strange, but if at all accurate, puts them well south of the Sugar Factory and close to Mount Cormont. At the same time the Commanding Officer of the *16th Hussars* discovered that he had just the *4th Squadron* with him and that his three other squadrons had disappeared. Lieutenant Colonel Ludendorf, realising what a dangerous situation the single unsupported squadron was in, ordered its return to Le Plessis-Chatelain. It searched for the other squadrons during its return journey but without success. On his return, Lieutenant Colonel Ludendorf reluctantly reported that he had brought back only a quarter of the regiment. Then, no doubt to his immense relief (or, more likely, to his immense fury), General von Garnier told him that he had kept the other three squadrons back as a reserve for his own purposes! This failure to keep the CO of the regiment informed of his plans seems to have been a habit of von Garnier's and may explain why the division broke up so easily during its later retreat.

The *15th Hussars* did manage to stay together, and made their approach further north of where the *16th Hussars* were supposed to be, and much closer to the German gun line. Initially they found an easier route down from the plain, and continued their charge until they almost crashed into the rear of the firing line of the *18th Dragoons*. Their headlong charge was only just stopped by the *17 Brigade* Adjutant, Rittmeister von Bredow. So, far from riding down British infantry, the hussars almost rode down their own dragoons! Lieutenant Colonel von Zieten then took his *15th Hussars* to the rear and dismounted them to assist the *18th Dragoons* with their dismounted attack. The encounter with the British infantry, which featured in General von Poseck's account, may perhaps refer to the repulse of the attack by the troop of the Queen's Bays led by Lieutenant de Crespigny, which cost the Queen's Bays many casualties. However, by this late stage of the battle it was becoming clear that British reinforcements were beginning to arrive, and von Zieten ordered the *15th Hussars* to withdraw to Le Plessis-Chatelain.

This final attempt to bring the weight of almost four cavalry regiments to bear on the southern flank of the Néry position seems

**Map 11. Final attack by 4th Cavalry Division as General von Garnier commits his reserve, the Hussar Brigade. All German guns are moved to south east position and General von Garnier commits his reserve brigade. However General Briggs strengthens his southern defences and 16th Hussars get lost in fog. 11th Hussars move their MGs to southeast corner.**

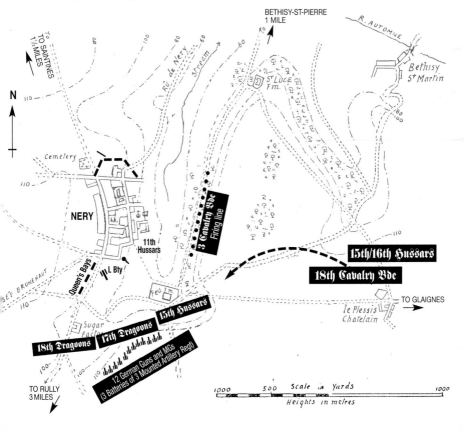

therefore to have been a total failure. However, the massing of guns and cavalry on the ridges south of Néry, combined with pushing men and machine guns into the sugar factory to support an attack on the Rully road defenders, must have appeared very threatening to 1 Cavalry Brigade. The German rate of fire may have slowed (possibly due to the casualties they had suffered and the need to conserve ammunition), but they would have had six Maxim machine guns to support the assault, and up to twelve 77mm guns (although probably a number of the guns and their crews may have been out of action due to damage caused by L Battery). The *17th Dragoons* and the four squadrons of the *15th Hussars* had moved forward on foot to support the gunners with their carbine fire, and this seems to have allowed the *18th Dragoons* to make a further attempt to get into the sugar factory. Initially they fired on the factory from their firing line, and then a patrol from the 1st Squadron of the *18th Dragoons*, led by two NCOs, Behnich and Gohrike, moved into some outbuildings of the sugar factory, and tried to get forward to the road and fire back at the Queen's Bays. According to the German accounts, this party was then attacked by enemy cavalry. This appears to have been a reference to the action by a squadron of the composite regiment of the Household Cavalry, which had come down from Mount Cornon and worked round to the sugar factory.

The cavalry attack was delivered by the 2nd Life Guards Squadron, which was leading the 4 Cavalry Brigade as it took up a blocking position on Mount Cormont (about 1.5 miles south of Néry). As it pushed one squadron forward towards the sugar factory, it was accompanied by a troop of the Royal Horse Guards led by Lieutenant P.V. Heath, who charged up to a body of the enemy (said by the Germans, to be the patrol from *1st Squadron*), which immediately fired at them. Lieutenant 'Volley' Heath was obliged to fall back and in getting away lost several horses and five men wounded. He himself was hit in the foot and leg, and while one of his men was trying to hoist him on his horse he was hit again, this time in the head. He died later in the temporary hospital in Baron and is buried there.

Leutnant von Muller then led quite a strong contingent from the *1st Squadron* of the *18th Dragoons* into the sugar factory and, perhaps at about this time, the dragoons also tried to bring two regimental machine guns into the factory buildings. According to an 11th Hussars' officer, the German troops were spotted trying to get two machine guns into the sugar factory to fire on the Queen's Bays and remnants of L Battery. Apparently the fire from I Battery managed to knock out these machine guns before they could do any real damage to the Queen's Bays, so it must have been fairly close to 8am when they were taken into the factory. As mentioned earlier, the sugar factory was not just one building, but a substantial complex consisting of several large factory buildings as well as a row of houses for the workers and numerous outbuildings. Although on a lower level than Néry, it could have provided ideal cover for an infantry force to dominate the Rully road and the southern end of the village.

L Battery had probably stopped firing by this time and the danger of being overrun was a distinct possibility. While Brigadier-General Briggs had available the three squadrons of the Queen's Bays and their machine guns, as well as A Squadron of the 11th Hussars, he appears to have called for reinforcements. Apparently, he sent orders for the two mounted squadrons of the 5th Dragoon Guards to return to Néry to meet this developing threat. He also ordered the 11th Hussars to extend their front to cover part of the northern end of the village, which released part of the 5th Dragoon Guard's C Squadron to move down to reinforce the defenders of the south of the village. In addition, the placing of the 11th Hussars machine guns on the south east corner of their defence line enabled heavy cross fire to be directed at the German guns.

To counter the build up of German forces in the sugar factory, a brave counterattack was then launched by a Queen's Bays troop of about fifteen men, led by Lieutenant Champion de Crespigny and Lieutenant Misa. The troop managed to get into position east of the factory, almost on the flank of the German guns. During this attack, Lieutenant de Crespigny was mortally wounded, as were many of the men. However, Sergeant Major Fraser continued to keep the Germans in check, so they could not get forward to the road. According to the account by Trooper Clark, only three men, including himself, were left unwounded at the end of this attack:

**Lieutenant Champion de Crespigny .**

*I was with a small party of about fifteen men who were ordered forward, and we reached the sugar factory and stopped a small German advance on that side. The Germans occupied some outbuildings. Lt de Crespigny and Lt. Misa led the counter-attack and Lt de Crespigny was killed. Misa, myself and one other man were the only ones to come out unwounded. I was incredibly lucky.*

According to the accounts by Frederic Coleman and Lieutenant de Labouchere, it was at about this time that the Germans used captured civilians, including the owner of the sugar factory and some of his workmen, as a human screen. Perhaps they were used against the attack by Lieutenant de Crespigny's men or when a group of Germans were escaping at the end of the battle. Coleman's account says:

> *Meanwhile the enemy had been gradually working round to the south and occupied the sugar factory.... Here they captured the owner and his workmen, whom they used as a screen against a party of the Bays under Lieut. de Crespigny. Several of the civilians were wounded and the Germans escorting them made off towards their own guns. These unfortunate civilians took cover in a beet field until they were eventually rescued by us at the end of the action.*

According to de Labouchere, about twenty five civilians were rounded up and forced to walk in front of some German troops:

**'Prince', drum horse of the Queen's Bays' mounted band.**

*The sun began to break through. The fog dispersed and made it possible to see the bottom of the valley distinctly, and the plateau of Sainte-Luce, the German batteries, and the regiments of German cavalry who, thanks to the fog, had been able to get so close to Néry. Then everyone was thunderstruck to see a column of Germans preceded by civilians advancing from the south and trying to come out from Néry sugar factory. Wasn't it perhaps only a stratagem? However, the civilians were avoided and fire continued on the Germans who followed them.*

**At this parade in York in 1919, veterans of the Queen's Bays commanded by Lieutenant Colonel Ing are inspected. Very few of those who went to France in 1914 survived to join this parade.**

These civilians included M. Levol, manager of the factory and Mayor of Néry, and his family. Others included M. Vasseur, manager of the beet-crushing plant at Néry, M. Henri Meignen from Verberie, and Mme Jeanselme, wife of a brazier at the factory. Lieutenant de Labouchere says he got fuller information about this incident from the Mayor of Néry, and while the British soldiers tried to avoid hitting the civilians, he discovered that there were some casualties amongst them:

*They made these unfortunate people walk in front of them hoping to protect themselves from the British fire. One man was wounded and a woman killed.*

This incident is not mentioned by any of the German accounts, and it is not clear who committed this crime against civilians. However, after the German gun position had been overrun by the 11th Hussars and the Middlesex Regiment, Leutnant von Muller and about twenty of his men, who had remained in the factory, tried to escape, were spotted and forced to surrender. Earlier, the machine gun officer of the 1st Middlesex, Lieutenant Jefferd, tried to get his guns down the Rully road to cover the factory, but his horse was shot under him and he was wounded by the Germans still in the factory and, as a result, the machine guns of the 1st Middlesex did not come into action. Finally a company of the 1st Middlesex and a dismounted squadron of the Queen's Bays cleared the remnants of the Germans out of the factory.

The Queen's Bays suffered a very serious level of casualties from the action that morning, due partially to their exposed position when the enemy shelling began and to their determination to carry the battle to the enemy and prevent the Germans from using the sugar factory to outflank 1 Cavalry Brigade. Their losses were almost as high as those of L Battery. Two officers and nineteen men were killed. The officers were Lieutenant Champion de Crespigny and Lieutenant Lynton Woolmer White of the King's Dragoon Guards, who was serving with the Queen's Bays when he was wounded. He died in the temporary hospital in Baron on 3 September and was buried there. Of the nineteen soldiers who were killed, most were buried at Verberie or at Baron. Also killed was one of the French interpreters attached to the Queen's Bays, Sergeant Bonvallet of the 6th Dragoons. This is a considerably larger list than the just one officer and eight men killed which Major Becke reported in his first account of the battle. This difference may be due to the large number of men who died from their wounds after the battle. Initially, more than thirty men were listed as wounded as well as eight officers including the squadron commanders, Major Harman and Major Ing; as well as the Adjutant, Captain Chance. This demonstrates clearly the brave and unselfish leadership shown by the officers. A few days later the regiment paraded seventeen officers and 423 men. Seven officers and 117 men were at that stage listed as dead, wounded or missing. Many of them were Néry casualties, which illustrates the heavy price the Queen's Bays paid in this action. After the end of the war of movement the regiment was often required to relieve units in the trenches and to operate as infantry when it often suffered severe casualties.

Justifiably the Queen's Bays (now amalgamated with the Kings Dragoon Guards as the 1st The Queens Dragoon Guards) regard their part in the action at Néry with huge pride. Like L Battery, they initially suffered shock and terrible losses as they were caught in the open by the German artillery. However, their speedy recovery and determination to fight back prevented the Germans from exploiting their initial success. The fire, particularly of the machine gunners, and the troopers along the Rully road inflicted considerable damage on the German cavalry and gunners and prevented them from storming the southern end of Néry, and indeed from retrieving most of their guns after they lost the initiative. Finally, the counterattack by Lieutenant de Crespigny and his men stopped the Germans from exploiting their build up in the sugar factory and ensured that 1 Cavalry Brigade was not outflanked.

# Chapter Eight

## REINFORCEMENTS ARRIVE

As soon as the attack on 1 Cavalry Brigade began, Brigadier-General Briggs had sent despatch riders requesting support to Major General Allenby at St. Vast, and Major-General Snow commanding the 4th Infantry Division at Verberie. The 4th Infantry Division had not been part of the original BEF but had come out to France some days later and had joined Lieutenant-General Smith-Dorrien and his II Corps just in time to take part in the Battle of Le Cateau. On 30 August, 4th Division and 19 Brigade were formed into the new III Corps. 19 Brigade had only been formed as an independent Brigade on 22 August from four of the regiments originally sent out as Lines of Communications defence troops. They were: 2nd Royal Welsh Fusiliers; 1st Cameronians; 1st Middlesex Regiment; and 2nd Argyll and Sutherland Highlanders. As a result there were more troops in the

**British Lancers on the march in 1914, still hoping to find a use for their lances.**

line but few troops available in the rear areas actually to guard the routes used by the BEF, which fact undoubtedly assisted *4th Cavalry Division* to escape later. 19 Brigade was located just north of Néry and 4th Infantry Division, with its three brigades, held the left of the British line. Briggs's messages were necessarily brief because, as the attack started in the mist, he had no idea of the size of enemy forces he was facing. Nevertheless, both commanders responded immediately and mobilised their forces to help 1 Cavalry Brigade.

Major-General Edward Allenby CB commanded the Cavalry Division. He immediately ordered 4 Cavalry Brigade, which was billeted nearby, to move the four kilometres towards Néry, and went with them together with his small staff. On their way they passed a composite infantry battalion from 10 Brigade, which had been ordered to march to Néry as fast as possible. The battalion had been formed by the amalgamation of parts of the 1st Royal Warwickshire Regiment and the 2nd Royal Dublin Fusiliers; and the men were in only their shirtsleeves, indicating the haste with which they had been paraded and ordered to move to Néry.

4 Cavalry Brigade, under Brigadier-General the Hon. CE Bingham CVO CB, had bivouacked in Verberie late on the evening of 31 August. The brigade consisted of the Household Cavalry Regiment, the 6th Dragoon Guards (Carabiniers) and the 3rd Hussars. In spite of the dense mist on the morning of 1 September, 4 Cavalry Brigade had already been alerted to something happening at Néry. They had, as usual, got up early and prepared for the continued retreat when they heard the sound of gunfire from the east, and felt spent rounds whizzing through their bivouacs.

At about 7am Allenby, together with Bingham and his staff, met Captain Osborne, the Staff Captain from 1 Cavalry Brigade, on the old Roman road to the west of the sugar factory. Due to the mist, which obscured much of the area, it was still difficult to appreciate fully what was happening. Therefore, (perhaps at the suggestion of Captain Osborne) General Allenby decided to assist 1 Cavalry Brigade by ordering 4 Cavalry Brigade to make a turning movement from the south of Néry to block and outflank the Germans.

The 3rd Hussars were ordered to support the advance of the composite battalion of the Royal Warwicks and the Royal Dublin Fusiliers with its B Squadron. B Squadron had some difficulty in locating the infantry (which shows how thick the mist was) but, when they were eventually found, the squadron covered their open right flank while the battalion advanced through the mist towards Néry, using the prominent chimney of the sugar factory as the direction marker. The rest of the 3rd Hussars were sent off to find and escort the batteries of the XXIX RFA Brigade, which had also been shelled in its bivouac north of Néry. Pivoting on the 3rd Hussars, the 6th Dragoon Guards were positioned about a mile east of Le Borde Farm. A Squadron was kept as a mounted reserve, while B and C Squadrons were dismounted and then advanced on foot towards the sugar factory. The infantry and dismounted cavalry advances arrived too late to take part in the action, although they would certainly have sealed the fate of the German cavalry if they had not already left the scene.

The third regiment of the brigade, the Composite Regiment of the Household Cavalry, was placed in a blocking position on Mount Cormont, which is the highest piece of ground south of Néry. Its 2nd Life Guard Squadron then advanced north to the sugar factory. It was closely followed by Lieutenant Heath and his troop of Blues, who attempted to charge a body of the enemy (almost certainly a patrol of dismounted *18th Dragoons*), and suffered casualties, causing them to withdraw. Lieutenant Heath was wounded in this action.

The artillery support for 4th Cavalry Brigade was provided by I Battery RHA. At this time the organisation of I Battery RHA was a little unusual. It had picked up an extra section of two guns belonging to D Battery, which had become detached at the battle of Le Cateau, and had managed to join I Battery a few days later. The Battery Commander, Major Thompson, had decided to split what had become an eight-gun battery, into two halves to make command easier. He had put his Battery Captain, Hugh Burnyeat, in command of two sections of I Battery to make a four-gun battery, and formed another four-gun battery from one section of I Battery and one section of D Battery, which he commanded himself. The field in which I Battery bivouacked also contained the VII Brigade RHA Ammunition Column, whose task it was to ensure resupply of ammunition for the two Batteries. It had actually bivouacked at Néry the night before.

Captain Burnyeat's four-gun battery came into action some 1,200 yards south west of the sugar factory at about 8am. The fire from the four guns of I Battery onto the German gun position really settled the matter with the German guns. Captain Burnyeat wrote to his brother, WD Burnyeat MP, about his part in the action at Néry:

*I commanded 4 guns of I & the major the other 2 guns of I &*

*the 2 guns of 'D'. We moved out of camp up the hill in the
direction of NÉRY where the firing came from, here I saw a lot
of Infantry in their shirt sleeves, they had been turned out of their
billets to go to the rescue & had not had time to dress, next I met
a party of the Queens Bays (2nd Dragoon Guards) all on their
feet & mostly wounded. Well I was sent up with my four guns to
the ridge in front & came into action in the open against a ridge
about 1200 yards in front where the German guns were, I could
just see the ridge through the fog.*

*Before I had time to open fire I was told that the position I was
in, in the open, was too dangerous & was to retire & take up a
covered position, I signalled to the teams to come up when the
Germans turned machine guns and rifle fire on us, I got the
teams stopped in time & when the fire slackened got them up
again & got the guns out of action; just as we were getting the
guns into action under cover we came under shrapnel fire from
the German guns. When we had got into action we were again
ordered to come up into the open which we did practically in the
same place we were in before, but with a loss of quite fifteen
valuable minutes.*

After Major Thompson had placed Captain Burnyeat's battery to his
satisfaction he went off to position his half of the battery, but was not able
to participate in the action before it ended. When Captain Burnyeat's
battery opened fire, some of the German guns swung round to engage
them. Fortuitously for I Battery, the position taken up by Captain
Burnyeat was near a derelict cultivator, and the Germans seem to have
thought this was an observation ladder for the Battery and directed most
of their fire at that point, thereby failing to damage I Battery.

*We started shelling the ridge & the Germans immediately
turned their guns onto us, however we had got the range of the
ridge their guns were on & silenced the remaining guns that
were firing on us. I got a message back to say that we had
silenced their guns & ordering me to bring a party to destroy
the German guns that had been silenced (eight in number),
also to send up six teams of horses to save & bring away L
Batteries guns.*

*I went up with eight men to the German batteries, our
dismounted Cavalry had in the mean time got there, & with the
aid of axes & pickaxes put the eight guns out of action.*

After looking at the German position, Captain Burnyeat crossed over
to the L Battery position:

*I then went across the little stream which divided the German Batteries from L Battery a distance of only 600 yds…here I met a horrible sight. L Battery had bivouacked in the open, the horses being tied to ropes stretching from gun wheel to gun wheel. They were actually harnessing the horses up when the Germans opened fire on them, their ammunition wagons containing their supply of ammunition were quite twenty yds from each gun. They had managed to get three guns swung round into action against the German batteries, but every round that was fired by L had to be carried by hand across an open shell swept space for twenty yards, they did fine work while they lasted*

**Map 12. British reinforcements arrive from the north and west and I Bty engages German guns. General von Garnier is forced to withdraw his battered division, leaving most of his guns behind.**

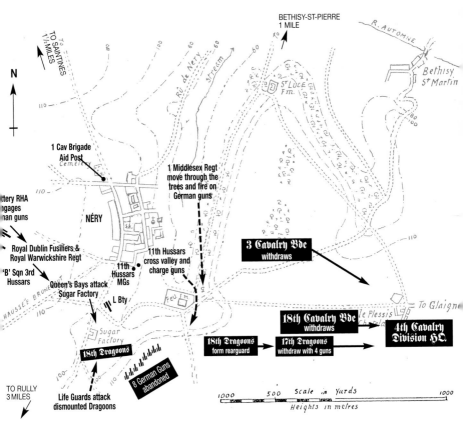

**German gun limbers abandoned during retreat.**

*putting at least 3 German guns out of action, but they were gradually all shot down,...The sight of dead men & horses that I saw when I arrived on the spot is better <u>not put into words. It was not a pleasant sight.</u>*

The intervention of I Battery's four guns had been decisive. It not only knocked out whichever gunners were still left in the gun position, but it also caught the German horse teams about 200 yards in rear of the gun position and made it impossible for them to get their guns out of the position. With their guns out of action and irretrievable, the German cavalry had no option but to withdraw and regroup as best they could.

Brigadier-General Briggs had also sent a messenger, advising that his brigade had been attacked by an unknown number of German cavalry in Néry, to 4th Infantry Division Headquarters (10, 11, and 12 Brigades) at Verberie, requesting support. 11 Brigade was at St. Sauveur, and it was ordered to move through Bethisy St. Pierre and take the German cavalry in the rear. 10 Brigade had already moved to support 1 Cavalry Brigade at Néry by the despatch of the composite battalion (Royal Warwicks and the Royal Dublin Fusiliers); although it did not arrive until after the 1st Middlesex, arriving from the north, had cleared the German gun positions.

19 Brigade, which was closest to Néry, had been ordered to advance between 10 and 11 Brigades. It had spent the night at St. Sauveur and by early morning had reached Saintines, (about one and a half miles north east of Néry). Lieutenant Colonel Ward of the 1st Middlesex was in temporary command of 19 Brigade. He ordered Major Rowley, temporarily commanding 1st Middlesex, to move at once to Néry and contact 1 Cavalry Brigade for instructions on how they could best help. Major Rowley set his companies marching to Néry, while he, with the leading company commander and machine gun officer, rode to join Brigadier-General Briggs at the north end of Néry. Briggs requested that they occupy the woods east of Néry and outflank the German firing line. As a result by about 8am leading elements of 1st Middlesex had arrived at the north end of Néry, then moved into the woods and began to open fire on the German gun positions. They were then close enough to join in the clearing of the German gun position, which had just been charged by C Squadron of the 11th Hussars. The Middlesex machine guns were able to cover a combined attack by a company of the Middlesex, commanded by Captain Gibbons, together with a dismounted squadron of the Queen's Bays, which then cleared the sugar factory, taking about twenty prisoners.

12 Brigade, acting as rearguard to 4th Division, had left the Royal Inniskilling Fusiliers to hold the outpost position north of Verberie along the River Automne. In that position they stopped *4th Cavalry Division* from escaping to the north and this led to the break-up of the division as it struggled to avoid contact with British forces by retreating southwards.

Despite achieving initial surprise and with repeated attacks by cavalry and artillery bombardment, *4th Cavalry Division* had failed to overcome 1 Cavalry Brigade and General von Garnier decided to abandon the field. He made his decision just in time. Had he not done so, the rapid arrival of so many British reinforcements would have resulted not just in the loss of its guns and prisoners, but the complete destruction of his division.

# Chapter Nine

# THE FINAL CHARGE AND CLEAN-UP

Once I Battery had commenced firing, the last of the German guns finally fell silent. The Germans then attempted to bring up horse teams to get their guns away. However, they came under fire from the guns of I Battery, and the machine guns of the 11th Hussars and the Queen's Bays. As a result, despite valiant attempts, they were unable to get the horses close enough to get all the guns away. Apparently, by prodigious efforts, the four guns of the most northerly battery were extracted, but the remaining eight were left in position. Brigadier-General Briggs then ordered the 11th Hussars to clear the guns with a mounted squadron. Lieutenant Colonel Pitman accordingly sent Major Lockett and his C Squadron to cross the ravine and pursue the enemy, who appeared to be retiring on account of the heavy machine gun fire and the accurate shelling of I Battery. Lockett had already ordered a dismounted reconnaissance of the far side of the ravine earlier in the battle, in case mounted action became possible. He had also ordered Second Lieutenant Curtis to try to contact the 5th Dragoon Guards, and he was able to signal from the far side of the ravine that it was clear for an advance.

C Squadron swiftly moved across the ravine, dismounted in half sections, with No. 3 Troop, commanded by Lieutenant Willoughby Norrie leading. The ground at the top of the ravine was secured and several Germans were captured. Parties of mounted and dismounted enemy were seen retiring eastwards over the plain. Lockett then ordered Norrie to charge the guns, while No. 2 troop opened fire on the fleeing enemy.

Lieutenant Norrie, like many other officers who took part in the action at Néry, later went on to a very distinguished military career and was eventually made Governor-General of New Zealand. As Lieutenant General Lord Norrie, he described his part in this exhilarating charge some fifty-three years later to the Royal Artillery Historical association:

> With drawn swords and a rousing cheer No. 3 troop galloped
> through the guns from the direction of Feu Farm. Quite a few of
> the shell-shaken personnel were still about and one was run
> through by my troop sergeant, Sergeant Hailey, for failing to put
> his hands up or shout 'Kamerad'...

A scene of the Battle of Nery based on a sketch by BSM Dorrell. It shows 3 British guns firing at the German guns on the far hill. The village of Néry is on the left of the picture and the Sugar Factory on the right. British soldiers are manning the sunken road across the middle of the picture and the Queen's Bays horses are shown panicking around the wooden shed, which was allocated to C Squadron.

*In point of fact there was little opposition and no organized fire but the occasional rifle shot. There were eight guns in position flanked by two machine guns. As far as I remember, five guns were pointing in the direction of 'L' and three in the direction of 'I'. After we had galloped through the guns, elements of the Middlesex Regiment soon arrived on the scene and Lockett quickly made a plan of action for the infantry to act as pivot from which we in 'C' Squadron could operate eastwards. The Middlesex Regiment were splendid and could not have been more co-operative.*

In fact an advanced patrol from the Middlesex had already got close to the German gun position and had been sniping at it from the edge of the ravine. They quickly joined the 11th Hussars in the German gun position and took charge of some twenty German gunners who were captured there. The 11th Hussars were under orders from Brigadier-General Briggs not to pursue the enemy too far as he was unable to provide any supporting squadrons. Nevertheless C Squadron, supported by three companies of the 1st Middlesex, was able to capture what was left of the Divisional Headquarters at Le Plessis-Chatelain, and to round up stragglers and bodies of enemy soldiers who were trying to hide from the British. The squadron was able to capture about 110 prisoners, including some forty wounded men, who were handed over to the infantry. Among those captured by Lieutenant Norrie were some of the medical staff at the Divisional Aid Post at Le Plessis-Chatelain:

*In Le Plessis-Chatelain we captured Germans from all six regiments of the 4th Cavalry Division, and also two doctors and two ambulances.*

*One of the German doctors protested when we removed his field glasses that they were a present from his girl-friend in Berlin. He also said his grey charger was private property and should not be taken from him. He even produced the Geneva Rules of War printed in French.*

*I should add I kept the field glasses myself and the grey charger was transferred to 'C' Squadron, 11th Hussars.*

Lieutenant Colonel Pitman provided corroboration of the German doctor's unsuccessful appeal to the protection of the Geneva Conventions:

*Amongst the prisoners taken were two doctors, with their ambulances and a number of wounded .... One of the German doctors was relieved of his field glasses and also of his nice-*

*looking grey charger; he protested violently that this was against
'the rules of war' and produced a book in German containing
extracts from 'the Geneva Convention'. He explained in French
that the glasses had been given him by a lady friend in Berlin,
and that he had bought his grey charger privately; that,
therefore, under 'the Geneva Convention', he was entitled to
retain his own private property and that it was most inhuman of
the 11th Hussars to have removed them!*

*Each doctor carried two loaded revolvers and each
ambulance contained two large boxes of ammunition – the Hun
doctor could not find a paragraph in the Geneva Convention to
explain this!*

Actually, although the medical staff and some wounded Germans were
taken prisoner, at least one account indicates that later some of the
severely wounded prisoners were left with their medical staff to be
picked up by the advancing German forces later that day.

Lord Norrie concluded his lecture by paying tribute to the dash and
endurance of the German cavalry:

*After this length of time, we can pay genuine tribute to the
performance of the 4th German Cavalry Division. They had
already covered 400 miles in three weeks and on August 31st
proceeded to march for twenty two out of the next twenty six
hours. On getting the information from his patrol, General von
Garnier gave the decision to attack immediately.... There was no
lack of dash by the German cavalry though there was certainly
lack of reconnaissance.... I thought nothing of the charge at the
time but it is historically correct that my troop were first on the
scene and captured the guns, the first to be taken in World War I.
The German guns had been silenced by the combined action of
L and I Batteries and the machine guns of the 1st Cavalry
Brigade, but someone had to reap the fruits of victory and it was
the good fortune of the 11th Hussars to have been there.*

However, Lord Norrie, like many of the cavalrymen at Néry, was
profoundly saddened by the death and mutilation of so many horses.

*After capturing Le Plessis-Chatelain and a number of
prisoners we were ordered to break the fight off and withdraw.
We returned to the scene of L Battery's historic stand and it is a
sight I will never forget. There were large numbers of dead
horses with their swollen bellies, and these were subsequently
buried by local inhabitants during the following fortnight.*

L Battery was said to have had 150 horses killed, while the Queen's

**Queen's Bays' C Squadron bivouac area near the cross-roads after the battle, showing huge pits where dead horses were buried by local villagers.**

Bays lost at least eighty killed, and a large number who ran away and were temporarily or permanently lost. Perhaps as many as 400 horses were lost by the British that morning. In addition the Germans had many runaways as well as many cavalry and artillery horses killed all over the battlefield, probably somewhere between 150 and 250 horses killed or lost. The local tradition is that the villagers had to dig pits for weeks after the battle to bury some 600 dead horses. More horses were lost that morning than in the Charge of the Light Brigade at Balaclava. Bombardier Frank Perrett summed up the feelings of many of the men as he recalled his worst memory of that morning in September:

*I joined the Horse Artillery because I was fond of horses and wanted to serve with them. But at Néry I wished I hadn't. It was bad enough to see your mates lying in agony, or blown to pieces; but at least they knew what it was all about, and no one made them join up. It was different with those poor dumb horses. I'll never forget one, a yard or two from where I was lying: both hind legs blown off, half sitting up on his mangled haunches, shaking his head and trying to struggle onto his forefeet. I was glad when a burst of MG fire finished him off.*

The fire in the L Battery field was so intense that close to 150 horses were shot down in their traces or blown apart, producing an immensely gory mess. As for the men, more than fifty-five were killed or wounded. Most of the fatal casualties in L Battery were caused in the initial shelling or among those men who bravely attempted to serve the guns. Fortune that morning was arbitrary. Sergeant Nelson was actually wounded three times, but still somehow managed to continue serving the gun. After he finished firing he picked up his jacket, which he had dropped close to the gun, and discovered, 'that it had received nine shots'. Most of his account of the action is laconic, but his description of the bloody scene of gruesome death and destruction around him is particularly vivid:

> *During the awful carnage the groaning of dying men and horses were audible amidst the terrific thundering of cannon, the scenes were in most cases beyond description. One man in full view of me had his head cut clean off his body, another was literally blown to pieces, another was practically severed at the breast, loins, knees and ankles. One horse had its head and neck completely severed from its shoulders. So terrific was the hail of shrapnel that I was bespattered with blood from men and horses, on one occasion as I opened the breech of the gun it (the breech) was covered with a mass of flesh and blood torn from the head of a dead man close by, this I had to wipe off with my hand before I could close the breech.*

The devastation caused by enemy shellfire and machine gun fire was so great that the miracle was that anyone in that field, let alone those serving the guns, survived at all. Gunner Darbyshire described the damage sustained by the F gun, which kept firing until it ran out of ammunition:

> *The side of the limber was blown away, the wheels were severely damaged, holes were blown in the shield, and the buffer was badly peppered by shrapnel bullets.*

Gunner Darbyshire was lucky to survive that day. He was relieved on the F gun by the heroic Lieutenant Campbell, who was then killed in the firing seat and he was stunned by the same shell explosion which took off the legs of Captain Bradbury, and caused his death. Driver Osborne who, like Gunner Darbyshire, was bravely risking death, fetching ammunition by crossing the open space between the gun and its ammunition wagons, was equally fortunate to escape death. Gunner Darbyshire described Osborne's 'lucky' injury in his account of the battle:

> *By the time we had practically silenced the German guns, the three of us who were surviving were utterly exhausted. Osborne, who was kneeling beside a wagon wheel, had a narrow escape from being killed. A shell burst between the wheel and the wagon body, tore the wheel off, and sent the spokes flying all over the place. One of the spokes caught Osborne just over the ribs, and knocked him over.*

Many men did their full duty that morning, and only some lucky ones survived to describe the events for posterity. The bravery shown all over the battlefield certainly deserved recognition. The Battery Commander, Major the Honourable Sclater-Booth, who was knocked unconscious as he ran back to the Battery and was unable to take any part in the action, was awarded the Distinguished Service Order.

Captain Bradbury, who inspired the Battery to resist and died a very painful death, was awarded the Victoria Cross posthumously. Lieutenant Giffard was awarded the Legion of Honour. Gunner Darbyshire and Driver Osborne were both awarded the Medaille Militaire. Battery Sergeant Major George Dorrell and Sergeant Nelson were both awarded the Victoria Cross. Lieutenant Mundy, who died from his wounds on 3 September, was apparently also recommended for the distinction, but it was not awarded. Certainly the award of three Victoria Crosses to the members of one unit in one action was an unusual event and acknowledged the bravery of many members of L Battery that morning.

Sergeant David Nelson VC.

All five of the battery officers were wounded in the action, and only Major Sclater-Booth and Lieutenant Giffard survived their injuries. Captain Bradbury and Lieutenant Campbell are buried together in Néry Cemetery and Lieutenant Mundy is buried at Baron. Originally, Major Becke listed twenty-nine other ranks as wounded and twenty of the battery killed. However, in addition to the three killed officers there are twenty-one names of other ranks recorded on gravestones in the area and no mention of Corporal Payne, who was reported to have been killed bringing ammunition to the F gun. Exact identification of bodies in the few hours after the battle, before the British vacated Néry, was difficult and in some cases impossible. For example, Major Sclater-Booth was fortunate to be found, still lying unconscious, by a rear party of the Queen's Bays. Corporal Payne's name is listed on the memorial at La Ferté sous Jouarre, with his death recorded as being on 4 September 1914. Remarkably, the two identical large memorial stones in Verberie and Néry, only record the names of twelve other ranks of the battery with seven buried at Néry and five buried at Verberie. This use of two memorials appears to be due to the fact that exact identification of all the bodies was not possible. In fact there are individual gravestones for up to eleven men who were apparently buried at Néry, and five more at Baron. Possibly some of the men who were listed as injured in the first count of casualties later died from their wounds. Anyhow, it would seem appropriate now to have a single memorial to record all the names of the twenty-five officers and men from L Battery who were killed in this outstanding action.

After the battle, most of the wounded, including many of L Battery, were taken to the temporary field hospital established in a chateau in Baron, some ten miles south of Néry. Sergeant Nelson says that there were some eighty British wounded in the hospital, as well as four French and twelve German patients. Possibly some German wounded may also have been left at Le Plessis-Chatelain, with their own medical staff, after the battle. The wounded at Baron should have been evacuated to a base hospital the next day, but this did not happen and, according to Sergeant Nelson, the Germans arrived that evening and made them prisoners of war. Even worse, the Germans took all their food! The next day those German, French and British patients who were fit enough were taken away in farm carts by a German officer, who undertook to return in a few days to collect more patients.

This promise of transport to imprisonment in Germany did not suit Sergeant Nelson who, despite a piece of shrapnel touching his right lung, was gradually recovering his strength. He therefore determined to embark on a classic 'Escape and Evasion' adventure.

*On Friday I was allowed up for two hours, this time I spent in a reconnaissance of the hospital compound, realising that as the German Guard of thirty men had eaten practically all our food, and very much to our dislike we were likely to go to Germany any day, something must be done to get relief either from the English or French.*

*On Saturday I had one biscuit for breakfast and was allowed up all day. I spent all the morning in keeping a sharp lookout on the surrounding country, when at about 1.00 pm I was rewarded by seeing a French Patrol riding near the hospital. Disregarding the strict orders that anyone attempting to leave the hospital would be shot by the German guard, I reached a low portion of the wall surrounding the Hospital, this I climbed with much difficulty as I could only use one arm, I ran in the direction of the French and succeeded in making them understand that there were many Germans on guard over about sixty English and two French wounded. The French lent me a horse and I rode with them during their reconnaissance, being fired on by some German patrols, which we encountered about two miles from Baron.*

*At about 9.00 pm I arrived at Plailly where I found the 14th French Division under the command of General Villaret. Finding a French soldier who spoke English, I asked to see the*

*General and explained to him the plight of my comrades at Baron, and he promised to send relief to them at an early hour on Sunday. I intended to accompany the relief party but was too exhausted to do so, therefore I am unable to state definitely whether my comrades are safe with the French or still prisoners.*

*At 4.00am on Sunday I left Plailly in an ambulance with the French Division and accompanied them until midday when I was transferred to a motor ambulance and sent to Dammartin, thence by rail to Sotteville-les Rouen, here I purchased some boots as the slippers in which I escaped were worn right through. At 11.00 pm Sunday I left Sotteville for a hospital, arriving at Dinan at 5.00 am on Tuesday – thirty hours of agony as each jar of the train caused a stinging pain in my side.*

The eventual fate of the wounded at Baron was far better than Sergeant Nelson feared. Even more remarkably they were the object of a VIP visit. According to Bombardier Perrett, after a few days in the Baron hospital:

*We were surprised by a visit from a German general and his staff. It was von Kluck. He asked if we were of the 1st Cavalry Brigade, and when we replied we were, he said he had heard that we fought bravely at Néry.*

Perhaps this visit to Baron by General von Kluck took place on 3 September, when he moved his headquarters from the Chateau at Compiègne to La Ferté Milon, and as a result could well have been in the Baron area. He certainly visited Crépy, just ten kilometres from Baron, and had an aperitif at the hotel 'Les Trois Pigeons'.

On that same day, 3 September, *First Army* had been despatched to march forty kilometres to the south-east to try to head off the French Fifth Army before it crossed the River Marne. However, not all of his army was in any condition to march. General von Kluck had been forced to allow *II Cavalry Corps* to rest for a day in the area close to Baron and reshoe its horses. He would, by the time of his visit to Baron, have known some details of the fate of the *4th Cavalry Division*, which was still reassembling at Droizelles and Versigny after its reverses at Néry, and had assembled only two of its brigades. However, he probably did not have had a full explanation of how a division, launching a surprise attack against a sitting target, had been overcome by just one enemy brigade. As Droizelles and Versigny are fairly close to Baron, perhaps he was in the area to visit *II Cavalry Corps* to check on the condition of its units, which were so critical for his success and also particularly to visit *4th Cavalry Division*. It is possible that he congratulated them on their bold effort, which could have had such a decisive influence on the campaign, if it had been

**The 9th Uhlans (Pommersches Ulanen - Regiment No.9) were on the right wing of the German attack at Néry. A British officer inspects one of their horses after the battle.**

more successful. Certainly his account of the action at Néry in his memoirs conveys the impression that *4th Cavalry Division* had actually carried out a successful attack at Néry, but was damaged when it came up against superior forces further south.

> *4th Division, after making a successful surprise attack on the enemy's bivouacs at Néry, became seriously engaged with superior forces near Rosières, north of Nanteuil-le-Haudouin, and incurred heavy losses.*

All of the accounts by German survivors of the battle accept that their attack against 1 Cavalry Brigade failed, although they ascribe this mainly to the resistance of the artillery and to the support which the Brigade received from flanking units. The author of the *18th Dragoons* regimental history actually quotes the RUSI account of May 1919 and goes so far as to claim that as the result of heavy losses the 1 Cavalry Brigade was effectively destroyed:

> *The English losses were extremely heavy... and due to its losses...the 1st Cavalry Brigade was actually as good as unbattleworthy.*

The reality was that 1 Cavalry Brigade had been damaged, but remained fully battle worthy and with Z Battery under command was able to play an immediate active part in the remaining part of the Retreat and the later British advance.

General von Kluck had hoped to achieve another signal Sedan Day victory by outflanking and destroying the whole of the BEF in its rest camps on 2 September, but the British Army had marched away in the night, before his pincers could close around them. So perhaps the sight on 3 September of so many wounded British soldiers from an apparent German victory at Néry was some consolation and continued to convince him that the British army was a spent force just waiting to be rounded up. It also seems very likely that it was as the result of this visit on 3 September that General von Kluck took the decision, later that day, to order a new and, as it turned out, crucial role for the remnants of *4th Cavalry Division*, which consisted of only two brigades at that time. The following morning *4th Cavalry Division* was placed under direct command of *IV Reserve Corps* and immediately sent two reinforced reconnaissance squadrons to cover the area north west of Paris (where the French Sixth Army was gathering to launch its attack on 5 September, thus beginning the Battle of the Marne).

Just a week later, the tide of battle rolled north again and the captive patients were released by a French infantry battalion, while the German guards were made prisoners themselves. Within a few days all the wounded had been evacuated to England. Only those unfortunates who did not survive their wounds remained in Baron. Lieutenant Mundy and five members of the battery still lie in the Communal Cemetery in Baron, as do eight troopers and an officer of the Queen's Bays.

Back at Néry, the rest of L Battery formed up under the Battery Sergeant Major and immediately got to work to cannibalise limbers and wheels so that the guns could be made ready to be got away. Colonel Drake, Commander Royal Horse Artillery (CRHA) of the Cavalry Division, had arrived and ordered Captain Burnyeat to take a party to destroy the German guns and send up six limbers to bring away the L Battery guns. Drake also ordered 37 (Howitzer) Brigade RFA to send some of its limbers to bring away any of the German guns that could be moved. In the event Captain Burnyeat decided that only three of the captured guns could be moved and these were then taken away and later displayed on Horse Guards Parade in London (although they were labelled as having been captured at Le Cateau). The remaining German guns were either already destroyed by gunfire or were put completely out of action with axes and pickaxes by the Middlesex soldiers and Captain Burnyeat's party.

Each of L Battery's six guns needed one or more new wheels, which were taken from the abandoned wagons and limbers. Some 150 horses were lost in the battle, out of an original strength of 228, and the survivors, together with those teams provided by I Battery, were sufficient to move all the guns. The surviving members of the battery, under the command of Sergeant Major Dorrell, and their guns joined

**Men of the Queen's Bays escorting German prisoners after Néry.**

the XIV Brigade Ammunition Column of the 4th Division's artillery and bivouacked with them that night. L Battery's guns were sent to the Army Ordnance Depot at St. Nazaire on 3 September. Sergeant Major Dorrell and the men moved down to the Army Ordnance Depot at Le Mans on 6 September, and were occupied fitting up guns, harness etc. until 17 October. On that date Sergeant Major Dorrell and one hundred and twenty four NCOs and men of L Battery entrained and left for England. They were welcomed back to the Artillery Depot at Woolwich at 8.45pm on 19 October by cheering crowds and the Royal Artillery Band. Within six months the Battery had been reformed and issued with 18 pounder guns and was ready for active service again.

Captain Edward Kinder Bradbury was awarded the Victoria Cross posthumously. The two surviving heroes of F gun, Sergeant Major Dorrell and Sergeant Nelson, were both awarded the Victoria Cross, and both were commissioned on 15 November 1914. Sergeant David Nelson was wounded in the leg, right lung, and ribs. He eventually recovered from these wounds and was presented with his Victoria Cross by the King on 13 January 1915. When he had fully recovered he was posted to the Shoeburyness Gunnery School. He returned to France and in due course was promoted acting Major. While commanding an RFA Battery he was wounded on 7 April 1918 and died of his wounds the following day. He is buried in Lillers Communal Cemetery. His widow presented his Victoria Cross to L Battery.

Battery Sergeant Major George Dorrell, who had joined the Army in 1895 when just fifteen, was commissioned on 15 November 1914 and married shortly afterwards. He was also appointed an acting Major in command of an RFA Battery in 1917. He retired from the army in 1921 and continued to serve in the Territorial Army. For a while he was the Adjutant of the London University OTC and was a Brevet Lieutenant

**Sergeant Major George Dorrell VC.**

Colonel. During the Second World War he served as a company commander in the Home Guard. When he died at the age of 90 on 7 January 1971 he was the oldest surviving VC holder and was given a military funeral by L Battery and The King's Troop RHA.

Bombardier Frank Perrett eventually recovered from his wounds, but had great difficulty in persuading a Medical Board that he was fit for further service. He had been so severely injured that he was only considered fit for light duties. He became a gunnery instructor at Woolwich for the rest of the war, before going out to Egypt with another RHA Battery. In 1931 he was given a quartermaster's job in a Territorial battery in the UK, and during the Second World War commanded a Home Guard unit as a captain, finally leaving the army in 1946. He died aged 78 in 1968.

L Battery was reformed and equipped with 18 pounder guns by March 1915. It took part in the Gallipoli campaign and then returned to France, where it served until the Armistice. Gunner (later Bombardier) Darbyshire and Driver Osborne were both killed at Gallipoli in 1915.

In 1926 the War Office approved the grant of specific 'Honour Titles' to individual batteries which had distinguished themselves in specific actions. Thus L Battery became L (Néry) Battery RHA. For a while, after reductions in the Army in the 1960s, it ceased to be an RHA Battery and became a Field Battery (due to 2nd Regiment RHA becoming 2 Field Regiment RA). On 1 December 1999 L (Néry) Battery was amalgamated with N Battery (The Eagle Troop) and became L/N (Néry) Battery (The Eagle Troop) as part of the 1st Regiment Royal Horse Artillery. Although amalgamation is always difficult to accept, both batteries had a similar history, having been originally formed in India, and had served alongside each other in many different campaigns over two centuries. Whenever possible, the battery continues the tradition of returning to Néry to commemorates that misty morning in September 1914, when Captain Bradbury called for volunteers, 'Come on! Who's for the guns?'

Meanwhile 1 Cavalry Brigade, having dealt with its casualties and having gathered as many of its horses as it could, then made its way south with the rest of the Cavalry Division. Having lost the support of its own L Battery, it was allocated the half battery of four guns commanded by Captain Burnyeat, promptly renamed Z Battery. Z Battery continued under the command of Captain Burnyeat and stayed with 1 Cavalry Brigade until it was replaced by H Battery at the end of September. During the night of 1 September, the Brigade bivouacked at Borest, just a few miles from the Forest of Ermenonville, not far from where the survivors of *4th Cavalry Division* were also making their way south to avoid potentially destructive contact with the British. During the night, *17 Dragoon Brigade* was forced to abandon some of its equipment and its remaining four guns, while nearby *18 Hussar Brigade* ran into the 4th Divisional Ammunition Park, resulting in a short firefight.

Although Néry was seen as an example of supreme heroism and eventual success for British arms, there were also questions raised about exactly why 1 Cavalry Brigade was taken by surprise. The initial success of the surprise attack reminded everyone of the importance of anticipating the worst. Perhaps 1 Cavalry Brigade allowed its tiredness to permit it to ignore the vulnerability of its position in Néry, particularly to a cavalry break-through. In retrospect the bivouac at Néry was particularly susceptible as there were no British defensive positions to the north of it (although Brigadier-General Briggs was unaware of that fact). Nevertheless, it is relevant to remember that combat would have been avoided altogether but for the morning mist, which caused Briggs to order a delay in the move-off of the Brigade. As a result of the mist and the delay order, 1 Cavalry Brigade should have paid a very high price for being caught unprepared in Néry by *4th Cavalry Division*. However, while it was obvious after the battle that it should not have relied for its external defence on other units, there is very little evidence that other units behaved any differently or that units which were not in the front line took greater efforts to protect themselves when they were in rear positions and the men were so tired.

Brigadier-General Briggs, with his experience from the Boer campaign, always stressed the importance of mutual defence, particularly in billets; and road guards and billet sentries were posted as a matter of course. Each of the Regiments sent out an early morning patrol to cover their areas of responsibility, and of course only in the east was there anything for Lieutenant Tailby's patrol to find. As the Germans were only just moving into attack positions in the mist, he could easily have missed them, so it was fortunate that he was able to spot them and raise the alarm. It is also not certain that 1 Cavalry Brigade could have achieved very much by posting picquets on the eastern approach and, as was realised at the time, it would have been difficult to support them. Nevertheless, Néry provides a classic example of how all ranks of the Brigade responded quickly when attacked. Not only did the senior officers demonstrate the strength of their leadership but clearly so did the younger officers and NCOs. Just as importantly, so did ordinary soldiers, who did what was necessary to feed the guns, carry water or rescue horses.

Briggs demonstrated outstanding cool thinking leadership

throughout the action. Firstly, although he was obviously surprised by the attack, he had the presence of mind to send off messengers immediately to request assistance from his divisional commander and 4th Division at Verberie. He then quickly made a plan to secure his defences, and created a reserve to deal with contingencies, while he attempted to regain the initiative by sending the 5th Dragoon Guards off to outflank the German attackers. He frequently visited all parts of his command during the action, walking to the north of the village to see Lieutenant Colonel Ansell depart on his flanking movement. He then walked down the defence line, with Major Cawley.

Having ensured that the flanks of the village were secured, General Briggs seems to have been most concerned to defend the southern side of Néry, where the most casualties were incurred and where he felt the enemy was concentrating his forces. Although 1 Cavalry Brigade was surprised by the Germans at Néry, and suffered many casualties as a result, the action ended decisively in its favour. Brigadier-General Briggs was later promoted and given further difficult tasks. As a Lieutenant-General he was sent to the very difficult Serbian Front in Salonika to command XVI Corps and was subsequently knighted.

The stiff British resistance at Néry, Villers-Cotterêts and Crépy on the morning of 1 September should also have provided a clear warning to the German commanders that the small British Army was in no way defeated, and remained a threat to their plans. The British, like the French, had suffered reverses due to the overwhelming numbers and firepower of the Germans. However, given a more even contest, the ability of the British and French to attack and defeat the Germans was unimpaired. The German reports stated that 1 Cavalry Brigade had been largely destroyed, when in fact it remained an effective fighting formation and actually went in search of *4th Cavalry Division* the next day. Both units required replacements for their artillery. However, 1 Cavalry Brigade received its new guns immediately and took its place as an effective element in the Cavalry Division later the same day. On the other hand, *4th Cavalry Division* needed several days to reform and did not become fully operative until 5 September.

Within six days of Néry, the BEF, whom General von Kluck had earlier claimed was 'retiring in disorder', was able to turn and so threaten the two pursuing German Armies that the Germans were forced to retreat to defensive positions on the Aisne and lost forever their best chance to defeat the Allies.

# Chapter Ten

# 4th CAVALRY DIVISION ESCAPES

By 9am, or perhaps even earlier, it was clear to General von Garnier that the situation was becoming very dangerous for his division. His apparently hapless enemy had not been overcome and was being strongly reinforced. He probably did not realise that elements of as many as four infantry brigades and another cavalry brigade were gathering to attack him, but more enemy troops were appearing and clearly it was becoming dangerous for his division to remain dispersed around Néry. He therefore decided to recall his units from their various attack positions as quickly as possible and concentrate his division.

**Map 13. Route of the 17th and 18th Mecklenburg Dragoons from the 1st to 4th September 1914.**

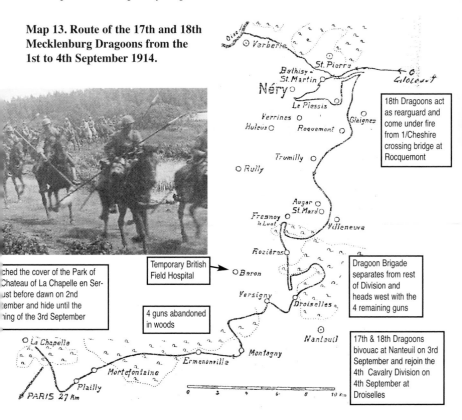

18th Dragoons act as rearguard and come under fire from 1/Cheshire crossing bridge at Rocquemont

Dragoon Brigade separates from rest of Division and heads west with the 4 remaining guns

17th & 18th Dragoons bivouac at Nanteuil on 3rd September and rejoin the 4th Cavalry Division on 4th September at Droiselles

Temporary British Field Hospital

4 guns abandoned in woods

...ched the cover of the Park of Chateau of La Chapelle en Ser-...st before dawn on 2nd ...ember and hide until the ...ing of the 3rd September

In any event, all units were recalled to Divisional Headquarters at Le Plessis-Chatelain, where most of the led horses were kept. To protect the area, the dismounted men of the *18th Dragoons* and the *Guard Machine Gun Battery* took up a defensive fire position to the south of Le Plessis-Chatelain. In their own account, the *18th Dragoons* say that they remained in action against the British until 2pm.

> *Reinforced by the 15th and 16th Hussars we were able to press forward to within 500 yards of the edge of the village, and might have mastered our opponents had they not received reinforcements during the morning...Nevertheless we were continually expecting help from the 2nd and 9th Cavalry Divisions, we held our ground until 2.00p.m. As the longed for assistance still failed us, we then had to withdraw, or else be destroyed.*

2pm is very much later than all the British accounts and perhaps they are referring to the time of their continued role as the divisional rearguard unit. It should also be remembered that German time differed from British time and was one hour later. The *18th Dragoons* were then recalled and remounted once the division was ready to move off, but continued to provide a rearguard for it as it retreated in a north-westerly direction, hoping to recross the Automne and reach the safety of the forest again.

However, as the division moved off, General von Garnier received reports that the crossings over the Automne were strongly held and shots were fired at his divisional reconnaissance parties from the other side of the river. They had probably run up against elements of 11 Brigade, which had been ordered to advance from Saintines to take the German attackers in the rear. Having been blocked on this route, *4th Cavalry Division* then headed east towards Glaignes, where it then received reports that the British were still in force at Crépy. This was a major disappointment. The division expected to meet elements of *First Army,* including the *Jäger* units, which had been due to attack and take the heights of Crépy early that morning. However, all the German attacks against the BEF that morning had made only slow progress and, as a result, *4th Cavalry Division* found itself surrounded by enemies and with no obvious escape route. The historian of the *9th Uhlans* summed up their dangerous situation poignantly:

> *Instead of friends we found only foes, who were marching in thick columns to the south.*

This lack of progress by *First Army* units forced another rethink. General von Garnier decided to strike southwest towards Rosières, where he might have hoped to meet up with the other two divisions of *II Cavalry Corps*. It is clear that not only was he out of contact with the rest of the Corps, but a major constraint to his actions was the lack of ammunition for his troopers as well as for the remaining four guns, which the courageous artillery commander, Captain Winckler, had managed to extract from the shambles at Néry. This meant that if he came up against major opposition, the division would be unable to fight its way through. He had little choice but to avoid trouble, if at all possible.

To avoid the enemy cavalry who might have still been on Mount Cormont, the division headed for Rocquemont, another village which, like Néry, was located on the edge of a steep and wide gorge. As the division passed to the east of the village, it was held up by a narrow bridge, which was the only way to cross the steep ravine outside the village. The four guns and the machine guns were got across first, and then the whole division crossed in single file. Just as the *18th Dragoons* were bringing up the rear, they were fired on, at some distance, by a company of the 1st Cheshires (from 15 Brigade). Apparently the advance guard of the division also got into a fire fight in Rocquemont, with a convey of British supply vehicles, and a number of dead and wounded Germans, as well as the looted vehicles, were later found by a reconnaissance party from the 1st Bedfordshires. The Bedfords also wounded and captured a German officer, who was accompanied by his orderly. He turned out to be Leutnant von Wiedebach und Nositz-Tankendorf, the Adjutant of the *2nd Cuirassiers*.

The division eventually reached Rosières at about 3pm. On its arrival it was very disappointed to discover no trace of the rest of *II Cavalry Corps*. After a two hour halt in the open to reorganise and tend to the many wounded, General von Garnier decided to find better positions for the division, and moved off. He was really fortunate in the timing of this decision because his divisional concentration had been spotted by the III Corps Report Centre just a mile away. As his division occupied an area almost two hundreds yards square it made a very tempting target. He moved off just in time to avoid being shelled by a battery of British 4.5in howitzers from 37 Brigade RFA (which, being wary of hitting unidentified friendly troops, took too long to come into action).

The *18th Dragoons* had now been designated as the advance guard. They left just before 5pm and headed south, with the four guns, towards Droizelles. The rest of the division split up into brigade packets and, instead of following the advance guard, passed into the large wood, the Bois de Roi, which lies to the east of Droizelles. The *18th Dragoons* were then recalled, and on their return they joined up with the *17th Dragoons*, who had been with the *18 Hussar Brigade* under the command of Major-General Count von Schimmelmann (although he normally commanded the *Dragoon Brigade*). This large column then moved into the woods east of Droizelles. At that point a staff officer caught up with them and relayed instructions to go to Versigny to meet up with the divisional staff.

However, when this large column got to Versigny there was no sign of the rest of the division. Reconnaissance parties were sent out and reported shortly that one British division was approaching via Baron (the 4th Division) and another British division via Nanteuil (the 5th Division). General von Schimmelmann immediately ordered the column to move to the east of the village, while he and his staff did a reconnaissance to the northwest. The two dragoon regiments, accompanied by the guns, were the first to assemble, and Lieutenant-Colonel Baron von der Heyden-Rynsch, the senior dragoon commander, thinking it was best not to loiter, decided to lead them off into the Forest of Ermenonville, part of the huge Forest of Chantilly, just to the west of Versigny. When von Schimmelmann arrived back, he decided to lead the rest of the party, largely the Hussars, but in fact comprising elements of every regiment, southwestwards towards Ermenonville. Thus the division was split up again into at least three parties. During the afternoon, von Schimmelmann's column captured part of the 4th Divisional Artillery Park in Ermenonville.

A divisional artillery park was a sizeable logistic unit consisting of eighty seven 3-ton lorries carrying sufficient ammunition to replenish the divisional artillery column. There was a firefight and some casualties. Certainly Private Davies of the Royal Army Service Corps was killed in Ermenonville that day and is buried, together with an unknown soldier, in the Communal Cemetery. Two British officers were also taken prisoner. Von Schimmelmann's column was very hungry but had no use for the British ammunition. However, this one incident alone clearly illustrates how dangerous a threat to the logistics and retreat of the BEF an undamaged and full strength *4th Cavalry Division* could have been. After some looting of the vehicles the Hussars spent the night of 1 September hiding in the forest until they were able to meet up with the advance guard of *First Army* on the following afternoon. Other parts of the division also began to gather at Droizelles and Versigny.

**German infantry resting on the line of march.**

Meanwhile von der Heyden-Rynsch was leading his dragoon party further into the forest. That night, as they made their way through the forest they could see all around them the bivouac fires of the retreating British units. They were actually not far from Ermenonville when von der Heyden-Rynsch decided that the risk of discovery and capture was so great that the Regimental Colours should be hidden and the four guns abandoned. The Colours were buried in a recognisable spot and they were just removing the breeches from the guns when there was a loud explosion. Apparently one of the guns had still been loaded when taken from Néry and there had been an accidental discharge.

Given the strong likelihood that British cavalry would come to investigate the explosion, there was no alternative but to recover the Colours quickly and, having buried the breeches, abandon the guns. The guns were covered with brushwood, and the exhausted column then made its way through Montagny and Ermenonville, without being stopped. A British cavalry unit from 4 Cavalry Brigade was ordered to investigate the report of enemy cavalry at Ermenonville and followed the trail of debris left by the column as far as Mortefontaine (just three miles from where the dragoons were sleeping), before deciding to give up the pursuit.

2 Cavalry Brigade also went in pursuit of German cavalry at about 2am on 2 September. They were also following up reports by locals that there were Germans in Ermenonville. As they moved through the forest from Mont l'Eveque, they found an area of the road littered with

saddles, equipment and clothing. Evidently a force had just decamped as they arrived. At that moment some shots were exchanged with a German rear party, but it got away in the forest. Shortly afterwards they discovered four guns, four limbers, an observing wagon and a pioneer wagon (marked *4th Cavalry Division*); all belonging to the *3rd Artillery Regiment*. The guns had the markings A.R.3, 2 and B4. These were the same markings as on the eight guns captured at Néry. In the event the cavalry did not have the horses available to tow the guns away, so they were destroyed in situ with explosive. Von der Heyden-Rynsch had been right to expect pursuit, but fortunately for his troops the British did not continue their pursuit.

The account by the *9th Uhlans* after the battle conveys the same impression as that of the dragoons of a disorganised and demoralised group of soldiers wandering around behind enemy lines desperately seeking to avoid being killed or captured. They had had no water or rest since leaving Offémont on 31 August, and badly needed both for the men and the horses. The *9th Uhlans* historian pointed out the unique nature of their situation:

> *The route led to the southwest – in reality direct to Paris – from whose outer forts we were only thirty kilometres away. It sounded so remarkable, that in order to save our lives and avoid being taken prisoner, we, fleeing, practically unbattleworthy German troops, were carried along in the middle of the defeated retreating enemy armies.*

Those who could rode any horse they could get hold of, but many of the men were forced to ride on requisitioned wagons. They were expecting to be captured at any moment and some of them made plans to break away and head north if they were intercepted by the enemy. Fortunately for the *9th Uhlans* they came upon a farm where many of their stampeded horses had collected and they were able to remount most of their troopers. At that stage they decided to leave their wounded in the care of the farmer. Actually some of these wounded were then taken to the temporary British military hospital at Baron, where the *9th Uhlans* account records that they later,

> *fell into the hands of the victorious German Corps.*

Whilst the British, escaping from the short hook of von Kluck's army on 2 September, feared a repeat of the overwhelming French defeat at Sedan, the Germans wandering through the woods were prey to their own similar fears. The regimental historian evocatively captures the suspense and fears of the fleeing dragoons:

> *Further and further rode the Brigade, the enemy bivouac fires*

*have long since died out. Ermenonville is traversed. Is it
occupied or free of the enemy? Apparently the enemy did not
think it necessary to have sentry posts so far behind the Front.
There was no challenge, but everyone expected a shot to be fired
which would signal the end. Hardly anyone dared to breathe. The
little village appeared endless. Finally the last houses...one is
again on the open road. A breath of relief goes through the
ranks... Any sense of time or distance is gone, half sleeping each
man sits on his horse and always the same worries, when will we
meet the enemy, and how long can your horse continue.*

Having passed Plailly, the column went on. It was challenged from a
house but gave no answer. Finally; just as dawn was breaking, the
column reached the park of the Chateau of La Chappelle en Serval.
Quickly the dragoons moved into the cover of the park. They replaced
the fence and hid all signs of their passage. They remained hidden and
sleeping in the park all day on 2 September and all that night, as the
sounds of retreating British and French troops passed them by. Some
officers went to watch the main Paris-Senlis road and saw long
columns of French troops hastening southwards all day: infantry,
artillery, cavalry and baggage all mixed up; clear evidence to them of
a defeated army in retreat. On the morning of the 3rd, it was quiet with
no sound of the enemy, and it was decided to push out patrols. One of
the patrols eventually met the advanced guard of the German *II Corps*
in Ermenonville. On its return the whole column mounted up and
moved to Ermenonville and eventually Nanteuil, where it was
delighted to meet up with its supplies. According to the historian of the
*18th Dragoons*, they:

> were greeted with enthusiastic hurrahs, as it had been
> rumoured that our Brigade (the 17th and 18th Dragoons) had
> been wiped out.

At last at Nanteuil the horses could be unsaddled and fed and, after the
men had eaten, they bivouacked for the night. Finally, on the morning
of the 4th, the Dragoons rejoined the *4th Cavalry Division* at
Droizelles. Other members of the Division came in that day. For
example two officers from the *9th Uhlans* appeared. Having lost
contact with their squadron on the 1st, they had survived for more than
sixty hours on just two tins of sardines and handfuls of berries.

The decision to attach the remnants of the *4th Cavalry Division* to
the *IV Reserve Corps* had already been taken, and two reconnaissance
squadrons (one from each of the Brigades that had already returned)
were sent off to Senlis and Creil before the dragoons rejoined the

division on the morning of the 4th. Four new guns were also provided that day, so that *4th Cavalry Division* could take the field with some artillery support the following day.

It has to be said that *4th Cavalry Division* was extremely fortunate to survive not only the action at Néry, but even more so the break up of the division and its wanderings through the villages and forests south of Néry in the following days. During this period, the retreating parties of German cavalry were constantly surrounded by overwhelming numbers of British and French troops. Given their lack of ammunition, they were very fortunate to escape contact. They were certainly seen from time to time and fired upon. Some groups and individuals were captured, but the great majority escaped without damage. Probably the division lost no more than thirty men to sundry incidents during this retreat.

Added to their problems was their extreme tiredness due to their pressing pace before reaching Néry, when they had spent twenty-six hours in the saddle. In addition they had very little sleep and almost no food or water for the men or their horses. As the author of the *9th Uhlans* account related, they were only too aware that the night of the 1 - 2 September was the anniversary of the great German victory of Sedan, but suffering greatly from hunger and thirst, and expecting to be found by the enemy at any time, their prevailing sentiment was much more akin to the great Prussian defeat at Jena.

Without doubt the delays imposed upon the German *First Army* on the 1 and 2 September, were invaluable in delaying and distracting von Kluck from his ambition to close with and destroy the French Fifth Army. Moreover, this delay was imposed with relatively little cost to the British, and this should have provided warning to the Germans that the men who fought so determinedly and gallantly at Néry, Crépy and Villers-Cotterêts provided little evidence of a defeated army. The British demonstrated clearly that, although retreating, they were still in fighting form and still a military force to be reckoned with. Notably, despite its significant casualties, 1 Cavalry Brigade was still operative and, to compensate for the destruction of L Battery, it was immediately allocated a temporary replacement; namely the half of I Battery (renamed Z Battery) with its four guns commanded by Captain Burnyeat.

1 Cavalry Brigade was therefore ready for action the same day. However, the immediate situation of *von der Marwitz's Cavalry Corps* was more serious. The elements of the *4th Cavalry Division* did not begin to reassemble until later on 2 September. According to the *9th*

*Uhlans* the whole of the division was thought to have been lost:

> *Due to the lack of signals equipment, communication with other German troops was impossible. The 4th Cavalry Division was considered by the Cavalry Corps to have been lost.*

Remarkably, General von Kluck decided to advance against the French on 3 September without *II Cavalry Corps,* which was given a day of rest, before joining the *First Army* advance on 4 September. However *II Cavalry Corps* then operated without *4th Cavalry Division*, which was still reassembling and had been placed under command of *IV Reserve Corps.*

General von Garnier's Division had been badly damaged, but had luckily escaped total destruction after its encounter with 1 Cavalry Brigade. Nevertheless, it was to play no further significant role in the rest of the German advance. As Lieutenant Colonel Poudret (of the Swiss Army) wrote in his review of the Combat of Néry:

> *It was a particularly warm affair for the German 4th Division. It lost there half its artillery, and was completely disorganised....*
> *The 3rd September was devoted, by the Germans, to re-establishing the Cavalry Corps; getting the units in order and shoeing the horses (thus a day was lost, at a time when minutes were of importance).*
>
> *As to the 4th Division, probably still suffering from its experiences, it was attached to the flank guard, the IV Reserve Corps, which was posted to the north of Meaux – that is to say, it was withdrawn from the front.*

*4th Cavalry Division* survived its encounter with 1 Cavalry Brigade and managed to evade the British forces sent after it, but was undoubted weakened by its narrow escape. It is therefore reasonable to ask exactly how badly damaged it was and how this affected its subsequent role in the German attack on France.

Early casualty estimates for many military actions are often wide of the final figures. Once bodies have been patched up and detailed records collected and sifted, the damage to the enemy always seems less than the successes claimed, and 'Néry' seems to be typical of this phenomenon. For example, Conan Doyle in his 1916 account of the action said that the Germans published their losses for the 'Combat of Néry' as 643 casualties (which he did not think was 'the complete loss, as the artillery does not seem to be included'), but unfortunately he did not quote the source for his number. Indeed in the same account he quoted the total British loss as, 'not far short of 500 killed and wounded'. Lord Ernest Hamilton, also writing in 1916, said that only

**German casualties left on the battlefield.**

three men from L Battery emerged unwounded. These high estimates can be contrasted with Becke's first list of German losses in his 1919 article; a total of seventy eight prisoners (includes only one artilleryman) and about thirty dead, with about 133 British casualties.

Brigadier-General Pitman's 1920 account includes the list made by the 11th Hussars, which he commanded at Néry. This account reports that there were very few German dead around the guns, but some twenty men were captured at the guns and as a result he suggests the total casualties for the Germans were the 110 captured (of which about forty were wounded) plus some forty dead bodies, which were counted after the battle. Assuming at least another 40 wounded, who escaped with the division, this makes a total casualty list of about 190.

In 1927, Major Becke, an artilleryman, who worked for the Historical Section of the Committee of Imperial Defence, produced a second, even more detailed, study of the battle and the progress of the *4th Cavalry Division* both before and after the Action at Néry. He depended largely on German sources for its new material. In this 1927 study he quoted figures provided by the Reichsarchiv, Potsdam, which showed the total losses as nineteen killed, forty one wounded and 102 prisoners making 162 altogether. Even these figures appeared incomplete and differed from those in some of the German regimental histories. Moreover, most British accounts state that between thirty and forty German bodies were left on the battlefield.

In particular, the Reichsarchiv figure for the losses by the Artillery of five killed and sixteen wounded and captured, appears very low when compared to the reports of artillery action by L and I Batteries against the German guns. The L Battery gunners were just 450 yards from the German guns and reported that they felt they had destroyed at least three guns. The British were firing shrapnel, which should have damaged the crews more than the actual guns. The fire of the battery and the machine guns was certainly sufficiently heavy to prevent the Germans from continuing to serve the guns or to move them. Captain Burnyeat, who came on the German gun position minutes after it was shelled mentions seeing:

> plenty of dead Germans and horses lying around the guns,
> 200 yds in rear there were heaps of dead and wounded.

Captain Burnyeat had deliberately fired at the area behind the guns in order to hit any gunners and their horse teams that might be attempting to get the guns away. It therefore seems very likely that the losses by the mounted artillerymen (who were only attached to the division) were considerably heavier than that stated by the Reichsarchiv.

All in all, the total casualties of *4th Cavalry Division* seem to have been of the order of over 200, with much of the difference from the Reichsarchiv total of 162 being due to an underestimate of the losses among the artillerymen, *17th Dragoons* and the *9th Uhlans*. In addition the division appears to have lost perhaps another thirty men during the flight from the British after Néry. As such the German casualties would appear to have been about twice those of the British.

However, a total list of casualties of even something close to 230 is far less than the *4th Cavalry Division* suffered at Haelen. Why, therefore, did the battle at Néry have such a deleterious effect on the Germans? Actually the *4th Cavalry Division* deserves considerable credit for showing far more energy and initiative at Néry than the other two cavalry divisions did with their attacks (at Verberie and St Sauveur) on 1 September, which hardly seem to have registered on the British defenders. Up until its defeat at Néry, *4th Cavalry Division* seems to have been enjoying its march through Belgium and France. There had been hard losses in Belgium, particularly at Haelen, which had taught them the limitations of mounted charges against infantry in good defensive positions. However, they had eventually triumphed and retained their strong morale as they looked forward to closing with the enemy in France and reaching Paris.

General von Garnier had launched his division in a blind attack against a sitting target, almost without any reconnaissance. In so doing he obeyed the injunction to be aggressive, and thus General von Kluck undoubtedly would have approved. In his book about the advance through France, von Kluck quoted appreciatively Caesar's maxim: 'In great and dangerous operations one must act, not think'. However, when this attack failed and the enemy showed an unexpected ability to fight back, von Garnier made successful efforts to extricate his division as best he could, although perhaps his success owed something to the poor pursuit by the British. His attempts to report his situation do not seem to have been very successful, probably due to his decision, the previous day, to leave behind some of his signals equipment. As a result the division was considered to have been 'lost' by *II Cavalry Corps* for at least thirty six hours after it passed Gilocourt.

What is clear from the regimental histories written by the Germans who were at Néry was the sense of fear, frustration and worry the tired troops felt as, after the unsuccessful attacks at Néry, they found themselves surrounded by overwhelming numbers of their enemies and, having abandoned their artillery, without the means to defend themselves. Their morale was badly affected and, as the author of the *9th Uhlans'* account says, it was a miracle that the division survived after the battle.

> *The English let us escape after the battle although it would have been easy for them to capture and destroy the German Cavalry Division which was surrounded by its Army. Even today each combatant of that ever-memorable day would consider it a miracle that the 4th Cavalry Division ever emerged from this trap into which it had put itself.*

The soldiers of *4th Cavalry Division*, hiding in the woods to save their lives, did not enjoy that experience and did not feel like members of an all-conquering army. They instead realised that they had apparently come up against overwhelming numbers of an undefeated enemy and their hopes of an easy victory had been snatched from them. This disappointment undoubtedly presaged the shock felt a few days later by the whole German Army, as its advance was halted within a short distance of Paris and it was forced to turn around and retreat north.

Undoubtedly the tough conditions of the German invasion through Belgium and France took a toll on both sides. The British, marching away from Mons and retiring on their own supply lines were often hungry and very tired, but gradually became hardened to the conditions and benefited from the occasional rest day. However, the Germans were not so well supplied and the constant riding and lack of sleep and supplies, which had been a problem since leaving Germany, was undoubtedly physically wearing down more than just the horses and their shoes. The German troops were extremely tired and their officers commented that only the certainty of eventual victory kept them going (helped by looted liquor!). For example, an officer in *First Army* wrote in his diary on 2 September:

*Our men are done up. They stagger forward, their faces coated with dust, their uniforms in rags. They look like living scarecrows…they march with their eyes closed, singing in chorus so as not to fall asleep… Only the certainty of early victory and a triumphal entry into Paris keeps them going… Without this they would fall exhausted and go to sleep where they fall.*

It was therefore a shock to find that the despised enemy could fight back, and eventually force the men of the *4th Cavalry Division* to flee for their lives. Perhaps it is too much to say that their morale was brittle, because the Germans were absolutely resolute when it came to fighting defensively, having been forced back to the Aisne; but certainly the transition from relatively easy victories to defeat and retreat was a blow to the morale of physically overstretched men.

In assessing the condition of *4th Cavalry Division* after the engagement at Néry, an interesting parallel can perhaps be drawn with the impact of the abortive charge of the British 2 Cavalry Brigade at Audregnies (near Élouges) on 24 August. The day after the Mons Battle, the BEF was attempting to withdraw south. The British 5th Division, holding the left flank of the BEF, was in danger of being overwhelmed by a powerful right hook delivered by von Kluck's *IV Corps*. All twelve battalions of the German *8th Division* pressed forward around Quiévrain to attack the British rearguard of just two battalions supported by the 119th Battery RFA, while the German 7th Division attacked around Élouges. On this occasion, to help the hard pressed 5th Division, Brigadier-General de Lisle ordered two of his regiments to charge towards the German *8th Division* (which was supported by nine artillery batteries) and halt its attack. This charge, by two squadrons of the 9th Lancers and three squadrons of the 4th Dragoon Guards, supported only by L Battery, may have startled the German infantry but certainly did not hold them up, as the cavalry never even reached the German infantry. Both regiments were severely damaged as they came up against wire fences, a railway embankment and shell and rifle fire and eventually had to escape as best they could, although L Battery was able to drive the infantry back by firing over the heads of the cavalry. As the Marquis of Anglesey states in his History of the British Cavalry:

*There seems little doubt that the actual charge was both inefficient and of little use. It was launched over 1,200 yards of virtually coverless and certainly unreconnoitred ground against an unknown number of infantry and guns… …The two regiments were so badly fragmented that it took some days before many of the survivors of the charge were accounted for. Meanwhile just when the 2nd Brigade was really needed to cover the retreat, it could only muster three squadrons instead of three regiments. The actual losses of the 9th and 4th were 169 killed, wounded and taken prisoner.*

Although the attack by the British brigade was much smaller, the actual losses suffered by 2 Cavalry Brigade were rather similar to those suffered by *4th Cavalry Division* at Néry, and illustrate the heavy impact such losses can have on the effectiveness of a cavalry unit in the immediate period following an abortive cavalry attack, particularly when so many horses had also been lost.

General von Kuhl (von Kluck's Chief of Staff), confirmed the weakened state of the division after Néry:

*the 4th Div suffered so heavily that on 4th September it was unable to advance with the rest of 2nd Cavalry Corps and he (von Kluck) is able to use it as additional strengthening of his open flank.*

Clearly he recognised that *4th Cavalry Division,* having shown so much boldness in its advance through British lines and in its attack on Néry, had suffered such losses that it was a seriously weakened unit. It swiftly received four replacement guns and was rejoined by its normal Jäger battalion. Nevertheless, even though it was able to mount an effective reconnaissance of the advance of Maunoury's Sixth Army towards the Ourcq on 4 September, it never became seriously involved in any of the major actions which ensued from 5 to 9 September. During the epic Battle of the Ourcq, when tens of thousands of men were killed and wounded, *4th Cavalry Division* manoeuvred on the periphery of events as it gradually retreated northwards. Perhaps it played an important role as a flank guard, but this involved very little real action, and it is noteworthy that it sustained very few casualties during this period. Commencing the action at Néry not only resulted in its relegation to flank duties, but seems to have undermined its fighting ability during a critical period when the German Army needed all available resources.

# Chapter Eleven

## IMPORTANCE OF THE NÉRY ACTION

It should be stressed that, although the action at Néry was extremely important for the soldiers who were there, it was only a microcosm in the Retreat from Mons. It involved a unit of just over 1,500 troops (out of a BEF of around 100,000), which suffered just 10% casualties. By comparison, just a week earlier, the British had suffered total casualties of almost 8,000 men at the Battle of Le Cateau. Even including a number of men who died from their wounds some days after the battle, making the final total number of officers and men killed fifty five (instead of the original estimate of forty two); the British losses of dead and wounded at Néry were still only about 135. 4 (Guards) Brigade suffered far more severe losses than this in the action that same morning in the woods north of Villers-Cotterêts, as also did 6 Brigade.

However, what distinguishes Néry from other actions during the Retreat was that it was the first significant encounter when the British remained in command of the battlefield after the action (if only briefly). They could savour an unexpected victory over an enemy who had surprised them and outnumbered them at least two to one. It provided the British with a brief opportunity to assess the damage their actions had caused to an enemy who, up to this point, seemed to be invincible, or at least impervious to the damage caused by the contact. It was extremely positive for general British morale to capture so many prisoners, as well as the whole of an enemy division's guns. As a result the British were encouraged in their belief that under the right conditions they could still beat the Germans. Even more importantly, the lesson of courage in adversity (shown particularly by the horse gunners), which turns defeat into victory, comes down through the years as an example to all soldiers.

For the cavalry of both sides, the attack by the German *4th Cavalry Division* provided affirmation of the critical importance of ground reconnaissance before charging blindly at the enemy. However, equally importantly, it confirmed the role of the cavalry as a strategic rather than a tactical weapon. The lesson was the same for the *4th Cavalry Division* at Haelen and Néry, and for the British 2 Cavalry Brigade, at Quiévrain (Élouges). It was that cavalry, no matter how brave, charging infantry (or dismounted cavalry) in defensive positions armed with modern weapons, would be cut to pieces. The development of modern weapons meant that the shock cavalry charge had ceased to be an effective battle-winner (except in very special circumstances). However, large cavalry formations foraying onto the flanks or even deep into the centre of the enemy, as at Néry, could destabilise the defence line and constitute a very effective threat, particularly among the 'soft' logistics units and bases.

Countering this threat could tie down large numbers of troops who were badly needed in the front line. Fortunately, *4th Cavalry Division's* encounter with 1 Cavalry Brigade at Néry rendered this particular threat impotent. *4th Cavalry Division* was extremely fortunate to be able to melt away afterwards and, although unbattleworthy, was able to secure its survival by concealing itself in the middle of the British retreat. Nevertheless, the numerous reports of German cavalry in the woods between the retreating British columns caused considerable panic in the rear areas. This perceived but unreal threat from the fleeing units of the *4th Cavalry Division* may actually have had a totally unintended benefit for the BEF, for it seems to have led to the decision to continue the general retreat on the evening and night of 1 September.

Frederic Coleman described the panic caused by one report:

> At half past seven on the evening of September 1st, panic orders came for a sudden movement of GHQ. The driver of a car came in with word that a body of six or seven hundred Uhlans had been seen in the vicinity. A never-to-be-forgotten scene was staged in the leafy lane. The big lamps of the cars sent long shafts of light through the gathering dusk. Hurried packing was done by everybody. Groaning lorries were forced up the steep drive. A detachment of cavalry and the bicycle company attached to GHQ, some foot soldiers, and a couple of lorry loads of Tommies hurried off together. No time was given to obtain food. Everything was helter-skelter. My car was the last out but one, and I left Dammartin with a sad realisation that my last remaining linen had been deposited that morning in Dammartin's sole laundry... GHQ sped on through the night as though all the German devils were on our trail. After what seemed an interminable time we reached Lagny.

Even though panic was denied, some British staff officers were left behind! Clearly there were several thousand German cavalry loose behind British lines on the night of 1 September, but they were actually just trying to stay out of trouble.

Whatever the real reason for the decision, British units were ordered to begin marching south during the night of 1 September. As a result, von Kluck's great encircling attack on the British on the 2nd, which might well have been catastrophic for the British, and would have totally pre-empted the Battle of the Marne, missed them completely. Frustrated by his lack of success, von Kluck then turned his attention back to the French and struck out for the River Marne on the 3rd. This continued exhausting forward march, in defiance of the orders from *OHL*, led to his disastrous positioning before the Battle of the Marne. Moreover, having largely wasted the 1st and the 2nd, he was too late to catch the French Fifth Army, which scrambled safely back across the Marne. Also, by marching at a tangent away from them, von Kluck allowed the British more time to recover, while stretching his own logistics and exposing his weak flank to the attack from Paris by the French Sixth Army.

Thus the generally unsuccessful attacks against the British by the immensely powerful *First Army* on the first two days of September wasted valuable time for the Germans, and allowed the French Fifth Army to escape across the Marne. Moreover the lack of tangible success against a 'beaten enemy' by *First Army* embarrassed von Kluck and caused him to take the fateful decision to seek a less ephemeral target, and to launch his army in a south-easterly direction against the flank of Fifth Army. Even more decisively, the 'scuppering' of *4th Cavalry Division* seems to have put an end to the ambition of General von der Marwitz and the 20,000 men of his *II Cavalry Corps* to threaten Paris. This took the pressure off the defenders of Paris and allowed the continuing build-up of the French forces which were to strike so effectively at von Kluck's western flank four days later. Despite the relegation of the weakened *4th Cavalry Division* to support *IV Reserve Corps* this added little to the real strength of *First Army's* flank protection. Apart from reconnaissance duties, *4th Cavalry Division* does not seem to have played any appreciable role in the largely static Battle of the Ourcq. Significantly, however, the absence of *4th Cavalry Division* weakened *II Cavalry Corps* by a third, and this was to impact adversely its efforts, as the rearguard force, attempting to slow the advance of the BEF into the gap between *First and Second Armies* after 6 September.

Without doubt all these positive outcomes for the Allies might well have been very different if 1 Cavalry Brigade had not drawn the teeth of *4th Cavalry Division* early on that fateful morning of 1 September 1914.

# Chapter Twelve

# LIST OF CASUALTIES

## British Casualties

Major Becke published a list of British casualties in his first account of the battle in 1919, based on the figures recorded in the DAA & QMG's diary of the 1st Cavalry Division. This list showed six officers and thirty six other ranks killed. In 1927, his revised list showed seven officers and thirty five other ranks killed and this figure has remained substantially unchallenged since then. However, when compared to headstones in the local graveyards, it does seem to have understated the British losses somewhat. This may have been due to the fact that some of the seriously wounded were captured briefly by the Germans and died before they were released. Altogether, the British seem to have suffered a total of at least eight officers and forty seven other ranks killed at Néry.

## Memorials

Against the western end wall of the Communal cemetery at Néry is a large, rather ornate, memorial to the four officers who are buried there. They are:

Major J.S. Cawley, of the 20th Hussars, killed at Néry, on 1 September 1914, aged 34.

Captain the Honourable Oswald Cawley, of the Shropshire Yeomanry, killed near Merville on 22 August 1918, aged 35.

(Oswald Cawley was the younger brother of Stephen Cawley. He was killed at Merville near Armentieres and his father, Baron Cawley, arranged for his two sons to lie together. A third son, who served with

**The Officers memorial in Néry Cemetery.**

**The memorial to the 12 soldiers of L Battery who were killed and buried at Néry and Verberie.**

the Manchester Regiment, was killed at Gallipoli on 23 September 1915 and is buried in the Lancashire Landing Cemetery at Cape Helles.)

Captain Edward Kinder Bradbury VC, RHA killed at Néry on 1 September 1914, aged 33.

Lieutenant John Davies Campbell RHA, killed at Néry on 1 September 1914, aged 31.

Also, as part of the obelisk, there is a stone memorial commemorating the award of the Victoria Cross to Captain Bradbury, Battery Sergeant Major Dorrell and Sergeant Nelson.

In the middle of the Néry cemetery there is a common plot for the soldiers of L Battery. According to a memorial stone at Néry and an identical one at Verberie Military Cemetery, twelve members of the Battery were buried in the common graves at Néry and Verberie; with five at Verberie and seven at Néry. In addition to the names of the twelve dead recorded on the individual gravestones in the special plots, there are a further four headstones in the Néry plot which seems to indicate that four more men are buried there, making a total of eleven in Néry and five in Verberie. Identification of many bodies was difficult after the battle and it is not clear exactly who lies in each graveyard.

### L Battery Royal Horse Artillery
*Buried or Commemorated at Néry Communal Cemetery*

| | |
|---|---|
| Captain | E. K. Bradbury VC RHA mortally wounded serving F Gun and died on 1 September 1914 |
| Lieutenant | J. D. Campbell RHA wounded serving C Gun, then killed serving F Gun on 1 September 1914 |
| 19380 | Serjeant D. P. Phillips RHA killed serving B Gun on 1 September 1914 |
| 56849 | Bombardier C. Martin RHA died 1 September 1914 |

143

| 39668 | A/Bombardier G. W. Richards RHA died 1 September 1914, aged 29 |
|---|---|
| 53525 | Driver A. E. Burtonshaw RHA died 1 September 1914 |
| 68866 | Driver E. Browne RHA died 1 September 1914 |
| 67928 | Gunner H. E. Bryant RHA died 1 September 1914, aged 21 |
| 70518 | Driver E. E. Collier RHA died 1 September 1914 |
| 55306 | Gunner W. E. Copplestone RHA died 1 September 1914 |
| 43374 | Shoeing Smith A. J. H. Heath RHA died 1 September 1914 |
| 63391 | Gunner P. Wornham RHA died 1 September 1914 |
| 29809 | Gunner T. W. Rae RHA died 1 September 1914 |
| 61503 | Gunner W. J. Richardson. RHA killed serving B Gun on 1 September 1914 |
| 519816 | Driver C. Mills RHA died 1 September 1914 |
| 32096 | Serjeant W. W. Fortune RHA mortally wounded serving D Gun, died 1 September 1914 |
| 53162 | Gunner A. Miller RHA killed serving C Gun on 1 September 1914 |
| 54307 | Driver S. Clayton RHA died 1 September 1914 |

*Buried or Commemorated at Verberie Military Cemetery*

| 19380 | Serjeant D. P. Phillips RHA killed serving B Gun on 1 September 1914 |
|---|---|
| 56849 | Bombardier C. Martin RHA died 1 September 1914 |
| 39668 | A/Bombardier G. W. Richards RHA died 1 September 1914, aged 29 |
| 53525 | Driver A. E. Burtonshaw RHA died 1 September 1914 |
| 68866 | Driver E. Browne RHA died 1 September 1914 |
| 67928 | Gunner H. E. Bryant RHA died 1 September 1914, aged 21 |
| 70518 | Driver E. E. Collier RHA died 1 September 1914 |
| 55306 | Gunner W. E. Copplestone RHA died 1 September 1914 |
| 43374 | Shoeing Smith A. J. H. Heath RHA died 1 September 1914 |
| 63391 | Gunner P. Wornham RHA died 1 September 1914 |
| 29809 | Gunner T. W. Rae RHA died 1 September 1914 |
| 61503 | Gunner W. J. Richardson. RHA killed serving B Gun on 1 September 1914 |

*Buried at Baron Communal Cemetery. A chateau at Baron was the site of a Field Hospital where many of the wounded from Néry were taken*

| Lieutenant L. F. H. Mundy RHA mortally wounded serving F Gun, died on 3 September 1914, aged 28 |
|---|
| 5596 Serjeant C. B. Weedon RHA died 8 September 1914, aged 36 |

| 33114 | Corporal F. S. Taylor RHA died 8 September 1914 |
| 64153 | Gunner E. T. Marsh RHA died 3 September 1914, aged 21 |
| 67611 | Gunner C. A. Gidney RHA died 8 September 1914, aged 20 |
| 68417 | Driver F. P. Tester RHA died 8 September 1914, aged 21 |

In addition, the accounts of the battle indicate that 34332 Corporal T. J. Payne of L Battery RHA was mortally wounded serving F Gun, but there is no indication of where he was buried. His name is listed on the memorial at La Ferté sous Jouarre, with his death recorded as being on 4 September 1914. This list of killed members of L Battery, gathered from the gravestones, totals twenty-five: namely three officers and twenty-two NCOs and soldiers (including Cpl Payne). This compares to the earlier quoted figure of three officers and twenty other ranks.

## 2nd Dragoon Guards (Queen's Bays)
*Buried at Verberie Military Cemetery in the common plot*

| 5557 | Sergeant G. D. Lewis Queen's Bays died 1 September 1914 |
| 5580 | Shoeing Smith C. Cram Queen's Bays died 1 September 1914 |
| 6328 | Private E. R. Bates Queen's Bays died 1 September 1914, aged 25 |
| 4580 | Private J. Dobson Queen's Bays died 1 September 1914 |
| 4471 | Private W. W. Fagg Queen's Bays died 1 September 1914 |
| 6452 | Private E. C. Felgate Queen's Bays died 1 September 1914, aged 22 |
| 5493 | Private A. J. Glanville Queen's Bays died 1 September 1914, aged 40 |
| 8050 | Private F. Wilson Queen's Bays died 1 September 1914 |
| 3251 | Private A. Smith Queen's Bays died 1 September 1914, aged 25 |
| 6339 | Private W. H. Withall Queen's Bays died 1 September 1914 |

Lieutenant Champion de Crespigny Queen's Bays died 1 September 1914. His body was probably buried at Verberie, but unusually was later exhumed and taken for burial in Maldon Essex.

In addition there is a stone marking the burial of eight unknown soldiers of the Great War in the common plot.

*Buried at Baron Communal Cemetery. Site of a Field Hospital where many of the wounded from Néry were taken*
Lieutenant Lynton Woolmer White, King's Dragoon Guards (attached Queen's Bays) died 3 September 1914, aged 28.

| 5947 | Corporal J. W. Turner Queen's Bays died 1 September 1914, aged 32 |

| 5378 | Lance/Corporal W. J. Turner Queen's Bays died 1 September 1914 |
| 4205 | Private H. J. Collins Queen's Bays died 1 September 1914 |
| 780 | Private Herbert Comerford Queen's Bays died 1 September 1914, aged 28 |
| 3514 | Private A. Farmer Queen's Bays died 1 September 1914 |
| 4941 | Private W. Norton Queen's Bays died 1 September 1914 |
| 7859 | Private G. H. Parkhouse Queen's Bays died 1 September 1914, aged 21 |
| 5438 | Private H. F. Richardson Queen's Bays died 1 September 1914, aged 21 |

Private Ellicock DCM Queen's Bays was mortally wounded serving the Queen's Bays's machine guns and died in hospital on 28 September 1914. He is buried at Portsdown Christchurch Military Cemetery.

This list of killed, gathered from the gravestones shows that the Queen's Bays suffered the loss of two officers and nineteen soldiers (including Private Ellicock), making a total of 21 killed; compared to earlier quoted figures of one officer and eight other ranks. It appears likely that some of those reported as being killed on 1 September, who were taken to Baron, actually died from their wounds a day or so later.

### 5th Queens Dragoon Guards
*Buried at Verberie Military Cemetery*
Lieutenant Colonel G. K. Ansell 5th Dragoon Guards died 1 September 1914. Killed leading the charge against the right wing of the German attack near St. Luce Farm.

| 599 | Private C. Lodge 5th Dragoon Guards died 1 September 1914 |
| D/5095 | Corporal R. Sherriff 5th Dragoon Guards died 1 September 1914 |
| 1 DG/6234 | Private W. S. Swymer 5th Dragoon Guards died 1 September 1914, aged 28 |
| 5992 | Private C. E. Yates (King's Dragoon Guards and 5th Dragoon Guards) died 1 September 1914, aged 30 |
| 7648 | Private A. W. Harrison 5th Dragoon Guards died 1 September 1914 |
| 866 | Private C. H. Miller 5th Dragoon Guards died 1 September 1914 |

The headstones at Verberie show that the 5th Dragoon Guards thus suffered the loss of one officer and six dragoons, but Major Becke's 1919 list has one officer and ten other ranks recorded as killed, which is corrected in 1927 to one officer and seven other ranks killed. Local tradition says that Lieutenant Colonel Ansell was buried initially near where he fell at St. Luce Farm, but his body was later moved to Verberie Cemetery.

## Royal Horse Guards
*Buried at Baron Communal Cemetery.*
Lieutenant Percy Voltelin Heath Royal Horse Guards died 4 September 1914, aged 26, was wounded leading his troop against the 18th Dragoons near the sugar factory at Néry and died of his wounds.

## Somerset Light Infantry
*Buried at Verberie Military Cemetery in the common plot*
6701 Private Margary Somerset Light Infantry died 1 September 1914 Private Margary is buried in the same mass grave as the other casualties of 1 Cavalry Brigade.

## Known German Casualties.
The following is a partial list of names extracted from the regimental histories. It is not known where these soldiers are buried.

## 9th Uhlans killed at Néry 1 September 1914
Ober Leutnant von Zitzewitz
Gefreiter Wilhelm Dahms
Ulan Gabriel Ostrowski
Ulan Karl Hensing
Ulan Johannes Behrens

## 18th Dragoons killed at Néry 1 September 1914
Leutnant Otto Heinrich Baron von Heintze
Sergeant August Labes
Unteroffizier Gustav von Puttkamer (died from his wounds several days after the battle)
Dragoner Friedrich Walter
Dragoner Otto Buhl
Dragoner Heinrich Drews
Dragoner Walter Wegener
Dragoner Heinrich Bape

## 15th Hussars killed at Néry 1 September 1914
Leutnant der Reserve Schoeningh

## 16th Hussars killed at Néry 1 September 1914
Gefreiter Heinrich Weiss
Husar Theodor Gluckstadt
Husar Emil Gradert (actually died on 3 September 1914)

# Chapter Thirteen

# LISTS OF GALLANTRY AWARDS FOR THE ACTION AT NÉRY

**Victoria Cross**
Captain E. K. Bradbury VC Royal Horse Artillery
Battery Serjeant Major G. T. Dorrell VC Royal Horse Artillery
Serjeant D. Nelson VC Royal Horse Artillery

**Distinguished Service Order**
Major the Honorable Sclater-Booth Royal Horse Artillery. Officer Commanding L Battery
Lieutenant A. J. R. Lamb 2nd Dragoon Guards (The Queen's Bays). Machine Gun Troop Officer

**Mentioned in Despatches**

| | |
|---|---|
| Lieutenant | Champion de Crespigny 2nd Dragoon Guards (The Queen's Bays). |
| Lieutenant | A. J. R. Lamb 2nd Dragoon Guards (The Queen's Bays) |
| Lance Corporal | F J Webb 2nd Dragoon Guards (The Queen's Bays) No. 1 on the first of the Queen's Bays' Machine Guns to come into action |
| Private | J Goodchild 2nd Dragoon Guards (The Queen's Bays) No. 1 on the other Queen's Bays Machine Gun |
| Private | Phillips 2nd Dragoon Guards (The Queen's Bays) No. 2 on a Machine Gun |
| Private | Fogg 2nd Dragoon Guards (The Queen's Bays) No. 2 on a Machine Gun |
| Private | Emmett 2nd Dragoon Guards (The Queen's Bays) No. 3 on a Machine Gun |
| Private | F. W. Ellicock 2nd Dragoon Guards (The Queen's Bays) No. 3 on a Machine Gun |
| Private | C. P. Horne 2nd Dragoon Guards (The Queen's Bays) carried ammunition and water to the Machine Guns |

## Distinguished Conduct Medal

| | |
|---|---|
| Sergeant | Longford 5th Dragoon Guards for action against the German 3 Brigade at St. Luce |
| Corporal | Peach 5th Dragoon Guards for action against the German 3 Brigade at St. Luce |
| Private | J Goodchild 2nd Dragoon Guards (The Queen's Bays) |
| Private | F. W. Ellicock 2nd Dragoon Guards (The Queen's Bays) carried ammunition to the Machine Guns and was wounded twice and later died in hospital |

## Legion of Honour

| | |
|---|---|
| Lieutenant | Colonel Wilberforce 2nd Dragoon Guards (The Queen's Bays) Croix d'Officier |
| Lieutenant | A J R Lamb 2nd Dragoon Guards (The Queen's Bays) Croix de Chevalier |
| Lieutenant | Heydeman 2nd Dragoon Guards (The Queen's Bays) Croix de Chevalier |
| Lieutenant | J Gifford Royal Horse Artillery. Severely wounded at Néry attempting to serve the B sub-section gun |

## Medaille Militaire

| | |
|---|---|
| Corporal | Short 2nd Dragoon Guards (The Queen's Bays) |
| Gunner | Darbyshire Royal Horse Artillery brought the F gun into action with Sergeant Nelson and continued to fire it and bring up ammunition |
| Driver | Osborne Royal Horse Artillery brought up ammunition to the F Gun |

# Chapter Fourteen

# TOURS OF THE AREA

Although it is more than 90 years since the events of this battle, a very good idea of the conditions which pertained in this part of France in early September 1914, can still be appreciated by a walk around Néry village and by a car tour of the local area.

The easiest approach to Néry is from the Calais-Paris autoroute at Junction 9, which is marked Creil. After the motorway tollbooth take the D122 just a short distance to the centre of Verberie, where restaurants and hotels may be found. In Verberie is also the military cemetery where many of those killed in the battle are buried, including Lieutenant Colonel Ansell and other soldiers of the 5th Dragoon Guards as well as the Queen's Bays and RHA. From the centre of Verberie follow the D932A up the hill out of Verberie. After crossing the new TGV bridge, take the first road on the left, the D26 signposted to Raray and Rully. After about a kilometre there is a junction with the D554 road to Néry. The approach from Verberie allows the visitor to gain a good impression of the route that the relieving troops from 4 Cavalry Brigade took when approaching Néry from the south west. At first Néry is totally hidden, but then, as the spire of the village church comes into view, it can be easily seen how the spire dominates the immediate area. This route from Verberie passes La Borde Farm and arrives at the main crossroads in Néry, opposite the L Battery field. On the left is a small memorial to the battle and L Battery, after which this crossroads is now named. On the wall behind is a memorial to the Queen's Bays who were quartered in these buildings and in the open field that was once here. Standing at this point between the L Battery field and the billets of the Queen's Bays, one can see the eastern ridge from which the first attack came as well as the sugar factory and the field stretching behind, where the German guns were located

## 1. Tour of Néry Village

The locations of most of the action, which took place in the area of the village, can be easily seen from a walking tour of the area around the village lasting about one hour. It is best to begin at the Mairie, where there are momentoes of L Battery and printed guides to the battle. Néry is a sleepy dormitory village, well away from the main roads.

There are no accommodation or restaurant facilities in the village, but visitors are always welcome.

Néry itself is a very old community, sitting astride an ancient Roman road, and with many buildings whose foundations go back at least until the Middle Ages. As the village is off the beaten track it has remained practically undisturbed by modern development and its main streets and buildings are still largely much as they were in 1914. Therefore it is easy to see where the action took place and imagine how vulnerable the men and their horses, stabled in the open, were to German guns firing from the high ground to the east. It is also obvious that those soldiers who had the good fortune to be billeted within the ancient farms were easily able to defend the thick stone buildings, and remain well-protected.

From the new Mairie, which is opposite the church, it is possible to walk between the two farms (which were defended by the 11th Hussars) and follow one of the overgrown paths down into the valley moving towards the far escarpment. The steepness of the western side of the valley and the steep escarpment in the east explains why it was so difficult for the Germans to get into the valley and how they could be easily seen and shot at by the dismounted cavalry and the two machine guns beside the church. The German *3rd Brigade*, which attacked from this eastern escarpment, was supported initially by one or two batteries of guns on the eastern ridge. If one follows the valley to the south (along gently rising ground) one can eventually come up beside Feu Farm. This was the route taken by the 11th Hussars for their

**Néry church today. The church has been restored but church services are now held irregularly.**

final attack on the German gun positions, which were in the open field between Feu Farm and the sugar factory. The factory and the factory houses are still in place today (although it now manufactures belting). From Feu Farm one can return to the bottom end of the L Battery Field and walk up the sunken road to the cross roads. In 1914, this sunken road was much lower and provided very good protection for the machine guns of the Queen's Bays and their firing line. The haystacks, which provided some protection to the gunners of L Battery, have now been replaced by a few modern houses.

From the L Battery crossroads one can walk back through the village (which still has a school but no working shops) towards the walled village cemetery, where many of the RHA lie buried. In particular, there is a memorial against the far wall to the Cawley brothers, Captain Bradbury VC and Lieutenant Campbell. In the middle of the cemetery is a memorial to twelve members of the Battery buried in the common graves at Néry and Verberie. However, as mentioned in the text, not all of the casualties have been recorded on the memorials and more men are buried at Baron municipal cemetery, including Lieutenant Mundy. A stone also commemorates the award of Victoria Crosses to Captain Bradbury, Battery Sergeant Major Dorrell and Sergeant Nelson.

## 2. Visit to the General Area

The significance of the attacks by the German *First Army* on the British positions in this area on 1 and 2 of September 1914 are often unremarked. However, it was the failure of those attacks at Néry, Crépy-en-Valois and Villers-Cotterêts to hold or destroy the BEF which later led to the destruction of the all the German hopes and their retreat to the Oise. Villers-Cotterêts, with its range of local hotels and restaurants, particularly an excellent Ibis hotel in the north of the town, provides a convenient centre for visiting the general area around Néry. A visitor to Villers-Cotterêts, which grew up around the hunting lodges of the French kings, should not miss the opportunity to see the ancient chateau of Francois 1. Today it is a retirement home, but by arrangement with the local tourist office the central chateau buildings can still be visited. Alexander Dumas was born nearby and his family chateau, which is now part of a camping site, can be visited at Villers-Helon, not far from the ancient Abbey of Longport, near where the German *2nd* and *9th Cavalry Divisions* rested on the night of 31 August 1914. There are good restaurants there too.

Just a mile north from the Ibis hotel, on the road to Compiègne in

**Guards memorial to those killed on 1 September 1914 on the side of the road in the Forest of Retz.**

the Forest of Retz, there is the poignant memorial to the guardsmen who were killed fighting in the woods on the morning of 1 September against the attack launched by the German *III Corps*. This was a difficult, savage engagement, as visibility and control in the woods were difficult. The Irish Guards had been formed on 1 April 1900 and this was their first major engagement. They were commanded by Lieutenant Colonel Morris, who was killed that morning and lies with many of his officers and some one hundred guardsmen.

This area has many historical connections with the First World War. Further north in the same woods is the memorial to the Observation Tower built by General Mangin. He used the Tower to launch the attack in the summer of 1918 as part of the Second Battle of the Marne, when the Germans, who had advanced almost to the Marne in their Spring Offensive, were finally driven back. Continuing northeast on this road towards Compiègne, past the impressive Chateau de Pierrefonds (which was restored by Napoleon III), brings one to Rethonde, near where the Armistice with the Germans was signed in 1918, and where the French were also forced to sign an Armistice in June 1940..

Journeying southwest from Villers-Cotterêts along the N2 and the N324 brings one to Crépy-en-Valois. This was the scene of the third major attack by the Germans on the morning of September 1. There, Jäger units from the *II Cavalry Corps* supported *IV Corps* in their attack on British positions. The attacks were not very successful and the British were able to withdraw in good order in the afternoon. The remains of the ramparts, with their imposing views, are certainly worth visiting.

From Crépy-en-Valois it is possible to follow the road through Duvy and Rocquemont to Néry or alternatively follow the N2 south to Nanteuil-le-Haudouin, from where the D330 leads to Baron. This is a small country road, which passes through Versigny and Droizelles, where *4th Cavalry Division* spent three days recuperating after its drubbing by 1 Cavalry Brigade at Néry. In the communal graveyard at Baron are the graves of the three officers and thirteen men who died from their wounds at the temporary military hospital established at Baron. From Baron take the D100 road due south to Montagny and then due west to Ermenonville. This follows the route taken by the German dragoon column as it fled from Néry and slowly wandered along the road through Mortefontaine and Plailly until they came to a hiding place in the park almost at the edge of the new Paris Motorway. Over the following ten days this whole area between Senlis and St Soupplets, was to become very familiar to *4th Cavalry Division* as it reconnoitred the area north of Paris and then manoeuvred on the outer wing of *First Army*, during which the latter was attacked for four days by the French Sixth Army in the bloody Battle of the Ourcq.

# BIBLIOGRAPHY

*History of the Great War, Military Operations, France & Belgium 1914*. Brigadier-General J E Edmonds, CB, CBE, CMG. Macmillan & Co. Ltd, London 1922

*The First Seven Divisions*. Lord Ernest Hamilton. Hurst & Blackett Ltd, London 1916

*Mons The Retreat to Victory*. John Terrain. B T Batsford, London, 1967

*August 1914*. Barbara W Tuchman. Constable, London 1962

*The Retreat from Mons*. Major A Corbert-Smith. Cassell & Co. Ltd, 1916

*From Private to Field-Marshal*. Field-Marshal Sir William Robertson GCB, GCMG, KCVO, DSO. Constable & Company Ltd. 1921

*A Military History of the War Vol 1*. Captain Cecil Battine. Hodder and Stoughton, London 1916

*The British Campaign in France and Flanders 1914*. Arthur Conan Doyle, Hodder and Stoughton, London 1916

*History of the Royal Regiment of Artillery*. Chapter 4. The Retreat to the Marne. General Sir Martin Farndale KCB. The Dorset Press, 1986

*A History of the British Cavalry 1816-1919*. The Marquess of Angelsey Leo Cooper, London 1996

*History of the First World War. B H Liddel Hart. Cassel & Co. Ltd 1970*

*The War the Infantry Knew,* Captain JC Dunn London 1938. Now copyright The Royal Welch Fusiliers Museum

*Tanks and Cavalry Tactics*. Brevet Colonel JFC Fuller, DSO. The Cavalry Journal, Vol X April- Oct 1920 (Page 125)

*The Menace to Paris and the Cavalry Action of Néry* (1st September, 1914). Captain de Labouchere, translated by Major A J R Lamb DSO. The Cavalry Journal, Vol. XXIV Jan – Oct 1934

*Paper by Lord Norrie entitled "The battle of Néry, 1st September 1914" delivered at the Royal Artillery Ballroom Woolwich 3 November 1967*. Lieutenant General the Lord Norrie, GCMG, GCVO, CB, DSO, MC. Proceedings of the Royal Artillery Historical Society Vol II No. 2. January 1968

*The Belgian Cavalry in the Combat of Haelen August 12th, 1914*. The Cavalry Journal Vol X April – October 1920

*The German Cavalry 1914 in Belgium and France.* Lieut-Gen Max von Poseck. Translated by Captain Alexander C. Streker and others. Berlin 1923

*The Action at Néry, September 1st 1914.* An account by an Officer of the 18th Dragoon Regiment. Translated by the Historical Section of the Committee of Imperial Defence with notes from "Mecklenburg's Sohne im Weltkrieg". The Cavalry Journal, Vol X April- Oct 1920 (Page 213-215)

*The attack on the First Cavalry Brigade at Néry, September 1st, 1914.* Brigadier-General T T Pitman, CB. The Cavalry Journal Vol X April – October 1920

*From Mons to Ypres with French.* Frederic Coleman. Sampson Low. Marston & Co, Limited 1916

*History of the Eleventh Hussars* (Prince Albert's Own) 1908-1934 Captain L R Lumley, Gale & Polden Ltd. Aldershot

*A personal account of the Battle of Néry by Gunner Darbyshire in I was there.* Vol 1, Edited by Sir John Hammerton, The Amalgamated Press 1938

*The Fight at Néry, September 1st,* 1914. Major A F Becke. The Journal of the Royal United Service Institution, Vol LXIV No. 454 May 1919

*Néry, 1914. Adventure of the German 4th Cavalry Division on 31 August and 1st September, 1914.* Major A. F. Becke. The Journal of the Royal Artillery, Vol LIV, No.3 1927-28

*The Guns of Néry.* J M Brereton (Includes the account of Bombardier (later Captain) Fred Perrett). Blackwood's Magazine No. 1935 Vol 3 21 January 1977.

*The Combat of Néry, (1st September, 1914).* Compton, Major T E The United Service Magazine, Vol LX New Series Oct 1919 to March 1920

*L Battery RHA at Néry, 1 Sept 1914.* Lt. Col H C R Gillman, MBE RA. The Journal of the Royal Artillery, Jan. 1954

*1914. Lyn Macdonald,* Michael Joseph, London 1987

*History of the Middlesex Regiment* Gregory Blaxland, 1977

*The March on Paris and the First Battle of the Marne 1914.* General-Oberst Alexander von Kluck, Edward Arnold, London 1920

*Personal letter by Captain H P Burnyeat, to his brother W D Burnyeat MP,* dated 28 September 1914. The Royal Artillery Historical Trust Collection RAHT MD/1428/2

Held at Firepower, the Royal Artillery Museum, Woolwich

*Personal account by William Thomas Clarke, a Trooper of the Queen's Bays* held by his daughter Mrs. Betty Field

*History of The Queen's Bays* Whyte & Atteridge
*Das 2 Grossherzogl. Mecklenberg Dragoner Regt. No. 18 in Weltkrieg 1914-18* Heribert von Larisch, Oldenburg: Stalling 1924

*Die Geschichte des Jäger-Bataillons 7.* Verein der Offiziere des ehemal. Kgl.Preuschen (Westfalischen) Jäger-Bns no. 7. Berlin 1929

*The Campaign of the Marne.* Sewell. Tyng. OUP, London 1935

*Geschichte und Gefecte des Husaren Regiments Nr. 16 1914-1920.* Offizieres Verein des Husaren Regiments No.16. Schleswig: Johs Ibbeken 1925

*A review of a book published in Paris by J. Hethay about the Role of the French Cavalry in the First Battle of the Marne* by 'M'. The Cavalry Journal, Vol X April – October 1920

*Battlefields of the Marne – 1914* Illustrated Guides to the Battlefields Michelin & Cie 1919

*Geschichte der 2 Pommerschen Ulanen Regiment No. 9.* Ernst Gunther von Etzel, Berlin 1931

*The Decisive Battles of the Western World Vol III.* Major-General J F C Fuller, CB, CBE, DSO. Eyre & Spottiswoode, London 1956

*Personal Account of the Action at Néry by Sergt D Nelson, VC (later Lieutenant, acting Major).* The Royal Artillery Historical Trust Collection RAHT MD/1428/1
Held at Firepower, the Royal Artillery Museum, Woolwich

*The Action of L Battery RHA at Néry.* Major P.F. Rodwell, RHA. The Journal of the Royal Artillery, Vol XCI No. 2 Sept. 1964

*Riding the Retreat.* Richard Holmes, 1995

*Field Note Book* of Captain Edward Sturgis Balfour, Adjutant of the 5th Dragoon Guards

*The 5th Royal Inniskilling Dragoon Guards.* Roger Evans. Gale & Polden Ltd. 1951

# INDEX

158

159